BUILDING
PORCHES
AND DECKS

FROM THE EDITORS OF **Fine Homebuilding**®

The Taunton Press

The Taunton Press
Inspiration for hands-on living™

The Taunton Press, Inc., 63 South Main Street, PO Box 5506, Newtown, CT 06470-5506
e-mail: tp@taunton.com

Distributed by Publishers Group West

INTERIOR DESIGN: Cathy Cassidy
LAYOUT: Susan Fazekas
FRONT COVER PHOTOGRAPHER: Ted Putnam
BACK COVER PHOTOGRAPHERS: Andy Engel, courtesy *Fine Homebuilding*, © The Taunton Press, Inc. (top left), Rich Ziegner, courtesy *Fine Homebuilding*, © The Taunton Press, Inc. (top right), Scott Gibson, courtesy *Fine Homebuilding*, © The Taunton Press, Inc. (bottom left), © Richard Lackey (bottom right)

Fine Homebuilding® is a trademark of The Taunton Press, Inc., registered in the U.S. Patent and Trademark Office

LIBRARY OF CONGRESS CATALOGING-IN-PUBLICATION DATA:
Building porches and decks / the editors of Fine homebuilding.
      p. cm. --   (Taunton's for pros/by pros)
Includes index.
   ISBN 1-56158-539-4
  1. Porches--Design and construction. 2. Decks (Architecture,
Domestic) --Design and construction. I. Taunton Press. II. Fine
Homebuilding. III. For pros, by pros.
   TH4970 .B863 2002
   690' .893--dc21

2002010194

Printed in the United States of America
10 9 8 7 6 5 4 3 2 1

The following manufacturers/names appearing in *Building Porches and Decks* are trademarks: Bear Creek Lumber™,Benjamin Moore®, Benjamin Moore® Moorwood®, Benajamin Moore® Imprevo®, Brock Deck®, Carefree Decking®, Certified Forest Products Council℠, ChoiceDek®, Coleman®, Color Putty®, Crane Plastics®, Inc., Cuprinol®, Cuprinol Revive®, CWF-UV®, Deckmaster®, Dow Corning®, Electrolux®, Enkamat®, Exolite®, The Forest Stewardship Council℠, Gougeon® Brothers, Kleenex®, Kmart℠, Lexan®, Midget Louver, 3M®, Olympic® WaterGuard®, Penofin®, Perma-Poly®, Plexiglas®, PPG Industries®, Pratt & Lambert® Permalize®, Sherwin-Williams® Woodscapes®, Sikaflex®, Sikkens®, Simpson Strong-Tie®, Sonotube®, The Southern Forest Products Association℠, Stripex®,Thompson's Water Seal®, Timber Holdings Ltd. Iron Wood Decking®, TimberTech®, TiteBond®, Trex Co.®, Velcro®, Wal-Mart℠, WEST System®, Wood Care Systems™, Woodguard®, Xerox®.

Special thanks to the authors, editors, art directors,

copy editors, and other staff members of *Fine Homebuilding*

who contributed to the development of the articles in this book.

CONTENTS

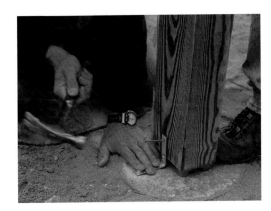

PART 4: DECKS: DETAILS AND DESIGN

INTRODUCTION

My memories began in a grand Italianate house that had a front porch, a back porch, and a screen porch. But in 1961 we moved into a new ranch-style house with a front stoop and a rear patio about the size of a blanket. The whole neighborhood was like that. Eventually people took to setting up their aluminum lawn furniture just inside the garage and relaxing under the canopy of its overhead door. It was a pathetic substitute for a porch, but it was better than nothing. You were sheltered from the sun and rain, and the garages all faced the street, so you could see what was going on and wave to people walking by.

So I learned early in life that it is better to have a porch (or three porches) than not to have one. But it wasn't until later, after I became a carpenter, that I learned how vulnerable porches are. I was always being asked to replace a rotten floorboard, tighten up a railing, or repair a torn screen. Exposed to sun, rain, and children, porches and decks take a beating. The right materials are critical, as are construction details that will shed water.

In this book, which is a collection of articles from *Fine Homebuilding* magazine, you'll find advice on materials and details, along with design ideas for all sorts of porches and decks. Written by builders and architects, who are discussing their own projects, these articles are the voice of experience.

—Kevin Ireton,
editor-in-chief, *Fine Homebuilding*

The original nondescript, split-level house (inset) was transformed with a new entryway. The new construction includes a roofed porch with a cedar-clapboard sunburst, an octagonal deck (at right), and a curving entry stair. The porch was built right over the old precast stairs.

Two Lessons from a Porch Addition

■ BY JAMES C. C. RICE

Everyone's heard the story of the drunk who stumbles into a house down the street because it looks just like his own house. I guess the neighborhood sot could have shown up at Ed and Loretta Korzon's place. Their split-level ranch was built during the suburban speculative housing boom of the late 1960s and was identical to the rest of the houses on the block.

In fact, the Korzons hadn't endured such an episode, and they might have had their front stairway to thank. Steep and treacherous, this precast stair pinned against the foundation was a struggle to climb—even while sober. The Korzons had pretty much given up using it. The basement shop door had become the primary entrance for the Korzons and their guests.

The Korzons wanted to use their front door again, so they hired me to design and build the covered porch with a curving front entry stair pictured here. Along with the gable-covered entry, I placed an octagonal deck in the northeastern corner of the porch. Its shape mimics a bay window on the house's north elevation. The deck offers a wonderful vantage point to view the distant hills and gives the house character. Laying out the octagonal foundation and devising a sturdy railing system for the octagonal porch were interesting challenges. In this article I'll talk about how I dealt with both.

Frame First, Foundation Second

The Korzon house occupies a dynamic, steeply sloped corner lot. Finding a way to lay out the new porch foundation accurately along the steep, irregular ground was the first problem.

Half the porch is supported on 10-in. piers. For the other half, including the octagonal deck, I designed a sloping octagonal retaining wall that returns into the existing foundation. Why a retaining wall? In the first place, I decided to build the new front porch over the old precast staircase. Only the top landing and the bottom two steps were removed. I wanted to use the material excavated from the pier holes to level out the ground below the porch and bury the precast stair. The retaining wall holds back this excavated material. Also, piers to

Laying Out a Tricky Foundation

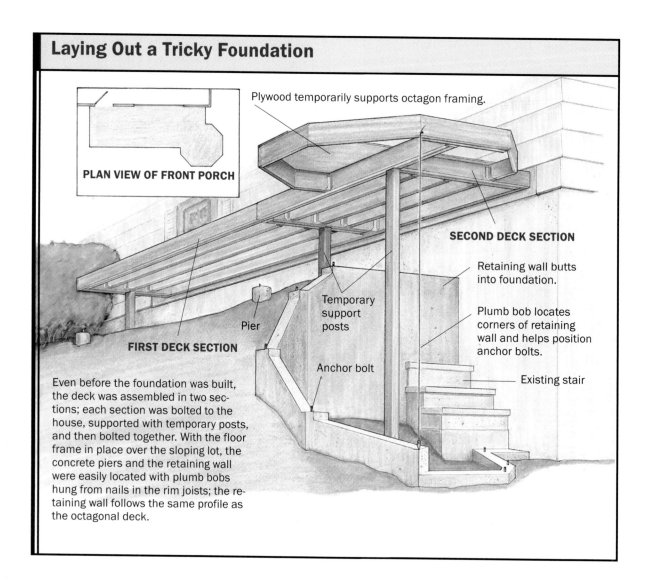

PLAN VIEW OF FRONT PORCH

Plywood temporarily supports octagon framing.

SECOND DECK SECTION

Retaining wall butts into foundation.

Plumb bob locates corners of retaining wall and helps position anchor bolts.

Existing stair

Anchor bolt

Temporary support posts

Pier

FIRST DECK SECTION

Even before the foundation was built, the deck was assembled in two sections; each section was bolted to the house, supported with temporary posts, and then bolted together. With the floor frame in place over the sloping lot, the concrete piers and the retaining wall were easily located with plumb bobs hung from nails in the rim joists; the retaining wall follows the same profile as the octagonal deck.

support each corner of the octagon would have been so close together that it was easier to dig a trench.

As I tried to figure out how to lay out the foundation, I realized how much easier it would be if the porch floor were already in place. Then I could just drop plumb bobs down from the framing to locate the piers and the retaining wall. Building the floor frame first would simplify the task of laying out the foundation. So now my problem was figuring out how to install the porch floor without a foundation to support it.

Framing the Floor

I could frame the porch floor most accurately by building it on the ground and raising it in two sections. To construct the section that includes the octagon, I built a template from two pieces of plywood screwed to some 2x4s. On it, I drew the octagon's framing, trim, and column and newel-post locations at full scale. The template reduced the math necessary to determine the length and shape of the framing members. Often I just scribed individual members right from the template.

The octagon cantilevers over the porch's rim joists, so I tacked a sheet of plywood on top of the floor framing to hold the octagon in place (remember, I didn't have a foundation yet). Then each section of the floor frame was lag-bolted to the house and to each other.

Temporarily supporting the edge of the floor frame was easier than I had imagined. Three 4x4 columns, 2 ft. in from the edge, did the trick and left me room to dig the pier holes and the trenches and to place the concrete.

After bolting the two floor sections together, locating the piers was easy. I started a few nails along the rim joist and hung plumb bobs.

I did the same for the retaining wall, which bears on a concrete footing. I dropped plumb bobs from each corner of the deck framing, measured 1 ft. to both sides of the bob and dug a circular trench below the frost line. The ground was firm, so it became the form for the footing.

When it came time to pour the retaining wall itself, I built forms to match the profile of the octagonal deck. The forms sat on the footing, plumb with the deck framing. To get the sloping effect in the retaining wall, I built hinged plywood doors at the top of the forms. As the forms filled with concrete, I closed the doors, tacked them shut, and continued the pour.

Finally, I used plumb bobs to locate the anchor bolts in each corner of the retaining wall and in the piers. Later, I attached galvanized steel post anchors and installed permanent pressure-treated posts to support the porch and the deck.

Shedding Water

The porch floor is 5/4 Douglas fir tongue-and-groove decking that runs perpendicular to the house. It's important to pitch exterior T&G decks because water cannot drain

Plumb lines at the deck corners help locate the foundation forms.

The posts were milled to continue the octagon down to the retaining wall.

through the joints. In this case, I installed the posts along the rim joist 1 in. shorter than level to facilitate water runoff. The posts supporting the octagonal deck were cut to match the same slope, and their faces were milled at 22.5° so that the trim below the deck would attach smoothly to the rough framing.

The decking was back-primed before installation. I let the decking run long, trimmed it to size, and routed the edges with a roundover bit. After sanding the surface, I finished the deck with two coats of Benjamin Moore® Moorwood® Deck Stain tinted light gray. This stain penetrates the grain and repels water like wax. It's a superior finish but requires annual reapplications.

Completing the Porch

With the decking installed, I was out of the hole, and the rest of the framing was straightforward. The 5-in-12 gable porch roof was framed on top of the house roof, and the outboard end rests on a built-up carrying beam and four 4x4 cedar columns. The new roof follows the same fascia and overhang lines as the existing roof, but it has a rake overhang.

I decided early on not to put a roof over the octagon because it's the section of the porch that stands highest above the ground, and a roof over this high section would overwhelm the rest of the house. The railing around the octagonal deck works much better with the sloping site because it serves as a stepped transition between the roofed section and the ground.

However, I couldn't put a column at each end of the roof because the one at the northeastern corner would land in the middle of the octagonal deck. Instead, I put a column on both sides of the octagon, and the roof's carrying beams cantilever over these columns. To balance visually the pair of columns at the octagon, I placed two columns on the other end of the porch.

Both pairs create thresholds—one frames the view, the other frames the front door.

After installing ⅜-in. Douglas fir ceiling bead and trimming the soffits and the carrying beams with clear cedar, I fabricated a sunburst at my shop and nailed it on the gable end.

Below the porch, I trimmed the rim joist, the posts, and the lattice in clear cedar. The square lattice I used was hard to find, but it works much better with the porch design than common diagonal lattice would have. With the bulk of the trim out of the way, I turned to the project's final challenge: building the octagonal balustrade.

Cable Strengthens Railing

Because an octagon is strong in compression but weak in tension, octagonal railings tend to be loose and rickety. The railing I built for the octagonal deck has square-cut handrails that butt into five-sided newel posts. I worried that this railing would loosen when people leaned on it. Then a light went on: How about a tension ring?

At the local marina I found plastic-coated stainless-steel cable and some flat-profile clamps; at the hardware store I bought two 4-in. stainless-steel eyebolts with nuts and washers, and at the plumbing supply store I purchased a short length of ⅜-in. copper tubing. I used the copper tubing as a sleeve to protect the wood fibers where the cable passes through the newel posts. I put the railing together and held it tight with a rope so that I could mark where the cable would enter the newel posts, which were not yet cut to length.

The newel posts are wrapped in clear pine; I made the wraps separately and slipped them over the rough newels. Next I set the railing sections (which I had pre-assembled) on 2x4 blocks between the newels. Then I scribed the posts (top left photo, facing page).

Cable-Tensioned Balustrade

Marking the cable hole. Railing sections were held between newels with a rope so that the newels could be marked and bored for the cable that strengthens the handrail.

A cable channel. The rough newel was cut to size; then a channel was routed for a length of copper tubing. The cable passes through the tubing to protect the wood from damage.

To cap it all off. Cut on a table saw from clear 2x8 cedar, the newel-post caps were sanded and varnished. A block screwed under the cap fits into the newel post.

Handrail conceals cable. This cedar handrail was grooved to hide the cable. Once the cable was tight, the handrail and a corresponding rail at the bottom of each section were fastened to the newels with galvanized 16d finish nails.

Anchoring the Tension Ring

The tension ring, a length of stainless-steel cable, is anchored at the columns that flank the octagon. The cable loops through the eyebolt and is clamped tight. Cable tension is adjusted with a socket wrench.

A tension ring is commonly built into the top plate of a circular building with a conical roof. The tension ring keeps the walls from splaying under the roof load. In the octagonal railing I built, the posts and the top and bottom rails act in compression, and the tension ring—a continuous steel cable threaded through the posts and anchored at the columns—provides tensile strength. People can lean against the railing until they cramp up, yet it stays tight.

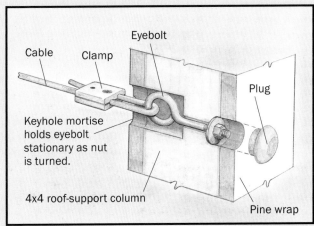

Cable

Clamp

Eyebolt

Plug

Keyhole mortise holds eyebolt stationary as nut is turned.

4x4 roof-support column

Pine wrap

The octagon's height and location make it a good lookout point, and the cable-tensioned handrail adds security. The corner of the porch roof cantilevers over columns that frame the view. The decking is 5/4 Douglas fir finished with a clear deck stain.

Anchoring and Tightening the Cable

Installation of the cable was a breeze. The cedar handrail stock I purchased has a milled groove on the underside (bottom left photo, p. 9). This groove was a fine place to conceal the cable. The cable runs beneath the handrail, through the center of the newel posts and ties to the two support columns flanking the octagon.

The cable is anchored at the support columns with eyebolts (drawing, p. 9). I scribed the entry point for each eyebolt shaft when the railing was held temporarily and then bored a hole. Above and below this hole I drilled others to make a keyhole mortise. This mortise prevents the eyebolt from turning as it's tightened.

I slipped in the eyebolts, threaded the nuts, passed the cable through the eyes and clamped it. I had to widen the channel under the handrail a little so that the clamp would fit. At the back of each column, I drilled a hole big enough for a deep socket; once the cable was tight, I popped in a finish plug. Then I used 16d galvanized finish nails to attach the top and bottom rails to the newel posts.

The finishing touch is a five-sided pyramidal cap on each newel post (top right photo, p. 9). I made the caps out of clear cedar 2x8 stock, sanded them, and finished them and the top and bottom rails with Benjamin Moore Impervo® 440 Spar Varnish.

James C. C. Rice designs and builds custom homes with Atlantic Contractors in St. Thomas, U.S. Virgin Islands.

I removed the railing sections; then used a ⅜-in. wood-boring bit to plunge through the wraps into the rough posts about ¼ in. The drill marked precisely where the cable threads through the rough posts. I slid the wraps off and inserted a short length of copper tubing in each one. Next, I cut the rough posts off directly above the ⅜-in. boring-bit marks. I then slid the wraps, with the copper tubing installed, back over the rough posts and traced the tubing's outline. I used a router with a ¼-in. straight bit to cut a channel for the tubing (top center photo, p. 9).

Porches That Won't Rot

■ BY KEVIN M. MAHONEY

Even as a boy, I'd happily go out of my way to look at a good porch. I'd ride my bike down the streets of old neighborhoods in Buffalo, New York, and imagine myself living in the houses I passed. My favorites were the houses with distinctive front porches. Massive and ornate or simple and elegant, the porch made the house.

I'm not surprised that I now work as a carpenter for a company specializing in building and restoring Victorian front porches. During the summer, we spend more than half our time either building new porches or fixing old ones. I think Garrison Keillor got it right when he described a good porch as a place that "lets you smoke, talk loud, eat with your fingers . . . without running away from home."

Because these open-air structures add so much to a house, I'd like the ones I build to last forever. That isn't literally possible. But we have developed a system for wood-porch construction that makes great strides toward that end. As we worked on older porches, it became obvious that what hurt them most was trapped moisture and lack of air circulation. That's what destroys columns, floors, and framing. Some builders of an earlier era avoided these problems by using hollow

At this Buffalo, New York, Victorian house, the front porch was rebuilt using techniques designed to eliminate trapped moisture that leads to rot.

posts and beams and by finding other ways to circulate air through the structure. We combine some of these time-honored techniques with a few of our own, and we add the protection that modern paints and sealants can offer. Our oldest projects, going back 11 years, still show no sign of decay, so we think we're on the right track.

Failure in the Usual Places

We rebuilt a porch for Robert and Denise Sheig in Buffalo. Their house is a beautiful turn-of-the-last-century Victorian that sits on a tree-lined street in the city's Delaware Park district. Parts of the original porch have held up for nearly 100 years; parts that failed were typical trouble spots. The wooden stairs and railings had long since deteriorated and had been replaced in the 1940s by concrete stairs and iron railings. The flooring below the columns and the bottoms of the columns themselves had rotted, as well as the spindle ends in the porch railing. The porch skirting had decayed where it pressed against the ground. And the porch beam and the exposed rafter tails had decayed where either the roof or the gutter built into the roof (called a Yankee gutter) had leaked.

Our first task was to rebuild the supporting posts and beams and the deck framing. After bracing the main roof beam from the ground, we removed old columns, railings, concrete stairs, and decking. About 50% of the existing floor framing could be salvaged; the rest had rotted beyond repair.

The floor joists rested on three 6x10 beams, 8 ft. on center (o.c.), running perpendicular to the house. The 6x10 beams, which slope ¼ in. per ft. so that water drains away from the house, were supported by rusting metal posts. After bracing the beams, we removed the metal posts; then we dug three 48-in. deep holes and poured in about 8 in. of concrete for footings. After the concrete had set, we added 3 in. of gravel for drainage, coated the new 6x6 pressure-treated posts

with Benjamin Moore Moorwood Penetrating Clearwood Sealer, and set the posts on top of the gravel in the holes. We topped off each hole with concrete and brought in some fill to pitch the grade under the porch away from the house.

The 2x10 floor joists, set 16 in. o.c., sit on top of the beams and are parallel to the house. We replaced the rotted joists with pressure-treated lumber. Normally, a 2x rim joist would be nailed to the ends of the joists to strengthen and stabilize the frame. But eliminating extra layers of wood reduces the chance of decay, so instead we used a 1x12 pine apron to cap the joist ends. The 1x12 serves the same purpose as a rim joist and also becomes the top rail of the skirting that we built later. This eliminated a layer of wood that might later hold moisture and lead to rot.

Along the front of the porch, the 1x10 pine apron had to be nailed to the face of the last joist. That couldn't be avoided, but we used ¼-in. thick furring run vertically 12 in. o.c. to separate the apron from its neighboring joist. We use this technique wherever possible: When two boards must be face-nailed, we separate the two with blocks or furring to encourage air circulation.

Deck Must Shed Water

Once the deck framing was complete, we allowed it to set for about 3 weeks before installing the deck boards. Pressure-treated lumber shrinks during this period, and decks can buckle if they are installed on new framing too soon. The 5/4 T&G flooring, 3 in. wide, runs perpendicular to the house so that water won't become trapped between boards as it runs off the deck. We painted the tongues and grooves with Benjamin Moore Alkyd Urethane Reinforced Porch and Floor Enamel and installed the decking while the paint was still wet. Painting the tongues and grooves is essential, but there is no reason to lose time waiting for those parts to dry. The paint provides a good bond between boards. We also coat the tops of all

Elements of a Rot-Resistant Porch

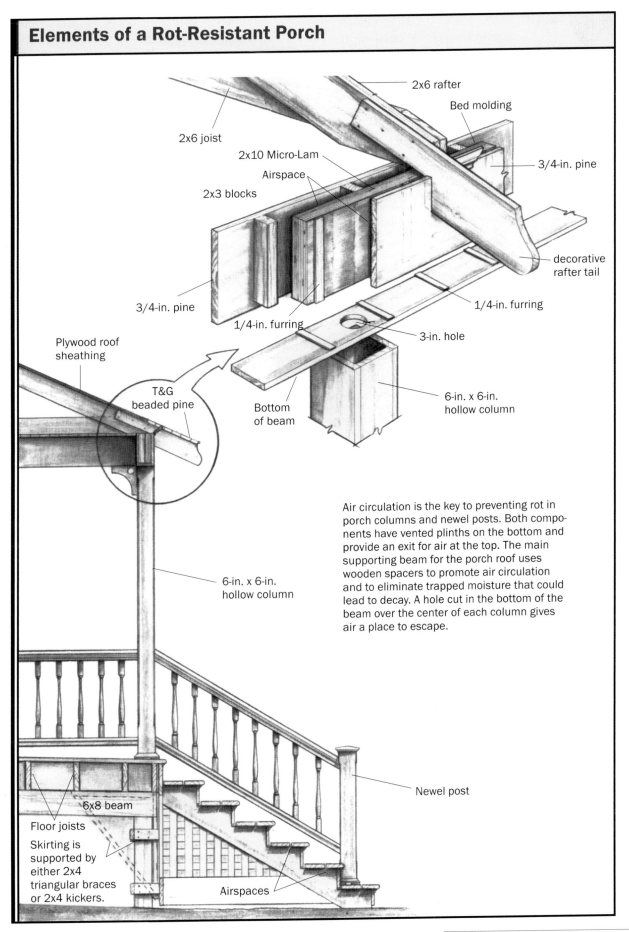

2x6 rafter

Bed molding

3/4-in. pine

2x6 joist

2x10 Micro-Lam

Airspace

2x3 blocks

decorative rafter tail

3/4-in. pine

1/4-in. furring

1/4-in. furring

3-in. hole

Plywood roof sheathing

T&G beaded pine

Bottom of beam

6-in. x 6-in. hollow column

6-in. x 6-in. hollow column

Air circulation is the key to preventing rot in porch columns and newel posts. Both components have vented plinths on the bottom and provide an exit for air at the top. The main supporting beam for the porch roof uses wooden spacers to promote air circulation and to eliminate trapped moisture that could lead to decay. A hole cut in the bottom of the beam over the center of each column gives air a place to escape.

Newel post

6x8 beam

Floor joists

Skirting is supported by either 2x4 triangular braces or 2x4 kickers.

Airspaces

floor joists with a penetrating sealer before the deck boards are installed.

Each deck board was blind-nailed at every joist with galvanized 8d ring-shank nails. We ran the decking long and then cut it off after installation, leaving an overhang of 1½ in. beyond the aprons. We rounded the edges with a router, sanded the deck, and finished it with three coats of the porch and floor enamel. We use oil-based enamel because it seems to dry harder and last longer than latex enamels, and it also has a high gloss we just can't get from latex paints.

Adding New Skirt Sections

The new skirting, which covers the gap between the porch deck and the ground, consists of frames made from ¾-in. lumber and either solid or lattice panels. Our skirts were designed to use minimal materials and allow maximum ventilation. And they maintain the original character of the Sheigs' porch. The top rail is the pine apron, 1x10 on the front and 1x12 on the sides (the side pieces

are wider so that the top edges can be tapered to follow the pitch of the deck). These pieces were fastened to the deck framing with 2-in. narrow-crown galvanized staples. The stiles are 1x8 pine, and the bottom rail is 1x8 pressure-treated yellow pine. The stiles and the rails are joined with biscuits, and the joints are backed with wood blocks glued with construction adhesive and stapled from behind. The support framing for the skirting was kept to a minimum to avoid a foothold for decay. We used either horizontal 2x4 kickers attached to the posts or triangular braces made from 2x4s.

The skirting on the original deck was a mix of lattice and solid panels, and we matched what was there. The solid panels are ¼-in. lauan mahogany plywood with two coats of WEST System® marine epoxy from Gougeon® Brothers, Inc. The marine epoxy doesn't raise the grain on the thin plywood panels and gives them added protection from the elements. The panels were coated on both sides and on the edges. We mounted them on the inside of the framework with ¾-in. galvanized staples; an ogee panel molding finishes the perimeter. The lattice panels were built in place using ½-in. by 2¾-in. pine strips, which we ran vertically and horizontally.

Building the Stairs

We cut our stringers from 2x12 pressure-treated yellow pine, which we buy in bulk and season for about a year before using. We set the stringers 16 in. o.c. and attached the top ends directly to the outermost floor joist. To stabilize the stringers and to prevent twist, we installed 2x4 blocks between the tops of the stringers but held the blocks away from the face of the joist with ¼-in. furring (photo, left). The bottoms of the stringers were set on a concrete pad pitched to carry water away from the porch. Once installed, the stringers were coated with two coats of the same preservative we used on the support posts.

A strip along the front of each stair tread gets a coating of epoxy and crushed walnut shells for good footing in poor weather. The furring at the top of the stairs will separate the top riser from the board beneath it and prevent trapped water that could rot the structure.

We used clear pine for both risers and treads because pressure-treated lumber is more susceptible to cracking and warping than clear pine is and because it doesn't have the same finished look as clear pine when painted. But we made the first riser from pressure-treated lumber because it rests directly on the ground. Risers are made from ¾-in. stock that is ripped so that the top edge supports the front edge of the next tread. We leave a ⅜-in. space between the bottom edge of the riser and the stringer to eliminate a water trap. The treads are made from 5/4 stock, two for each step. We also leave a ³⁄₁₆-in. gap between the two treads and between the risers and the adjoining treads so that water will drain easily. To provide sure footing, we epoxied a strip of crushed walnut chips on the front of each step. The chips are manufactured by Buffalo Sand Blasting Sands Company, Inc. We use size 10-12 chips and find they work better than anything else we've tried.

A New Main Beam and Roof

We had hoped to save most of the original hip-roof framing and the supporting beam. But we ran into more rot than we had expected—a typical renovation dilemma. We stripped five layers of leaky roofing and removed the 1x8 plank sheathing, which had rotted in spots, and badly at the edges. The decorative rafter tails had deteriorated and so had the decorative T&G beaded-pine sheathing used on the overhanging portion of the roof. The front section of the beam had taken water from above, and because it was made up of sandwiched 2x8s and wrapped tightly in ¾-in. pine, the beam had trapped the water and rotted.

To get the strength we needed and still have a relatively hollow front beam, we used a 2x10 Micro-Lam (a laminated plywood beam), which ran the entire length of the porch. To build it out to the necessary finished dimensions, we glued and screwed

2x3 blocks to one side of the Micro-Lam and then glued ¼-in. vertical furring to the other side. We also furred the bottom of the beam with ¼-in. material, and then wrapped the sides and the bottom in ¾-in. pine to match the existing side beams.

We drilled a 3-in.-dia. hole in the bottom of the beam where it would rest on each of the 10 columns. The holes would allow air circulation between the hollow columns and the beam and roof framing. We cut new rafter tails from clear pine, sealed them with two coats of WEST System epoxy and installed them. New 3-in. T&G beaded pine was run on the top of the rafter tails where it could be seen from below. From this point up, where the sheathing would be hidden by the porch ceiling, we used ¾-in. CDX exterior plywood. We used 30-lb. felt and asphalt self-sealing three-tab shingles to finish the roof.

Vented Columns and Newels

To me, installing columns and newels is the most enjoyable part of the job. This is what brings neighbors out of their houses and what seems to invite people to stop their cars and visit. The ten, 8-ft.-tall, 6-in. by 6-in. columns and the four 3-ft.-high, 6-in. by 6-in. newel posts were made from ¾-in. clear pine. The posts are simply long boxes primed on the inside and stapled together with galvanized 2-in. narrow-crown staples.

The trick to keeping air moving through both the columns and the newel posts is wooden plinths we make ourselves. Making the plinths takes time, but they add a finished look to our porches (compared to commercially available metal vented plinths), and we can make them any size we need. We start with a base made from shaped 5/4-in. by 2½-in. clear pine. We miter and spline the corners and glue the base together with epoxy, leaving a square hole in the middle for air to enter. We glue four 2½-in.-square by ½-in.-thick blocks to the bottom corners for feet. To the top of each plinth we then glue two blocks of wood that slide into the posts and prevent lateral movement. Once completed, each plinth gets two coats of marine epoxy. Although I don't do it, some builders install screening at the bottom of the plinth to keep out pesky insects.

The four plinths that anchor the newel posts have a ⁷⁄₁₆-in. hole drilled through each corner. First we fill these holes with epoxy, and when it is dry we drill smaller holes through the epoxy for mounting screws. This effectively creates an epoxy gasket that prevents moisture from entering. We use galvanized 3-in. drywall screws to mount the newel plinths to the deck and the stairs. The plinths used under the columns are held in place by the weight of the porch roof and the beam.

Newel posts also need to be vented at the top, just like the columns. We start with a ¾-in. plywood subcap for each newel; we cut these to overhang the newels by ³⁄₁₆ in. on each side. We then cut a 3-in. semicircular bite out of each side of the subcap. A 1-in. wide ogee molding hides the edges of the subcaps. A beveled cap made from ¾-in. clear pine is then fastened to each subcap, with a ⅝-in. overhang on all sides. Construction adhesive alone is used to install the finish caps to eliminate any nail holes and possible water infiltration. Once assembled,

Newel-Post Construction

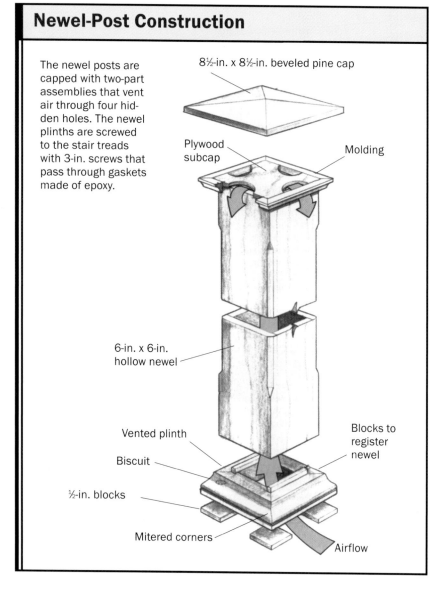

The newel posts are capped with two-part assemblies that vent air through four hidden holes. The newel plinths are screwed to the stair treads with 3-in. screws that pass through gaskets made of epoxy.

8½-in. x 8½-in. beveled pine cap

Plywood subcap

Molding

6-in. x 6-in. hollow newel

Blocks to register newel

Vented plinth

Biscuit

½-in. blocks

Mitered corners

Airflow

each cap gets two coats of marine epoxy inside and out.

When we are done, we have created a passageway for air to enter plinths at the bottom of columns and newels, travel upward and be vented at the top. This eliminates trapped moisture inside columns and newels and helps prevent rot.

New Railings and Rinish

Once all the columns were built and installed, we took measurements for the 12 railing sections. For this porch, we used relatively standard railing components available from local suppliers. We started with turned spindles 1¾-in. square at top and bottom. They were sealed, sanded, and primed before assembly.

The spindles were spaced approximately 4 in. o.c. and held together at the top with ¾-in. by 1¾-in. subtop rails and on the side with stepped molding. On top of that assembly, we set sections of beveled top rail and sealed it with two coats of marine epoxy. To hold the bottoms together we sandwiched the spindles between two pieces of 2½-in. by 1¹⁄₆-in. shingle molding. Water can't collect around the bottom of the spindles, and air can circulate freely. Railings are installed about 4 in. off the porch deck and are toenailed to the posts with 8d galvanized nails. The three long sections of railing were supported with 4-in. high pressure-treated blocks wedged between the deck and the bottom rails. We took care to seal the end grain on all components before installation.

We primed most of our components with an oil-based exterior primer before installation. This gave the parts some protection and stability during the four-week construction phase. After completion we filled the nail holes with glazing compound and brushed and sprayed on two coats of Pratt & Lambert® Permalize® Alkyd Gloss House

and Trim enamel. Our only concern was painting the epoxied components, but paint adheres well to a sanded epoxy surface.

Kevin M. Mahoney is a carpenter and supervisor with Victorian Restorations in Buffalo, New York, who also runs his own home-inspection business.

No Trapped Moisture in Railings

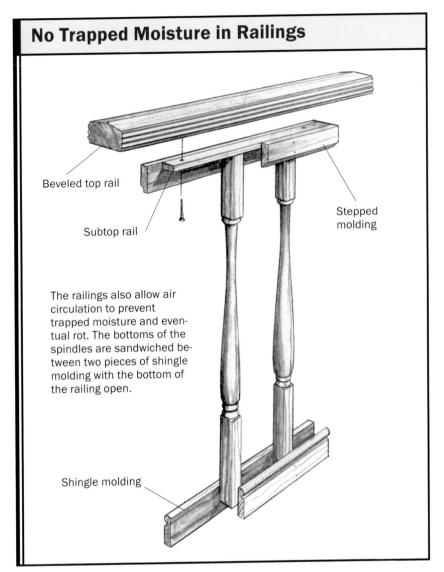

Beveled top rail

Subtop rail

Stepped molding

The railings also allow air circulation to prevent trapped moisture and eventual rot. The bottoms of the spindles are sandwiched between two pieces of shingle molding with the bottom of the railing open.

Shingle molding

Sources

Gougeon Brothers, Inc.
100 Patterson Ave.
P.O. Box 908
Bay City, MI 48707
(989) 684-7286
www.gougeon.com
WEST System marine epoxy

Pratt & Lambert
101 Prospect Ave.
Cleveland, OH 44115
(800) BUY-PRAT
www.prattandlambert.com

Without the porch, the three-story brick walls made this house look stark and barren. The porch provides a graceful skirt around three sides, turning barren into beautiful.

Building a Grand Veranda

■ BY KEVIN WILKES

Our clients' home was a nineteenth-century three-story manor near the banks of the Delaware and Raritan canal in central New Jersey. Built for the owner of a nearby rubber factory, the house had triple-wythe exterior brick walls 12 in. thick. The house also boasted a large porch that wrapped around three sides.

In its second century, the house began to show its age and needed significant repairs. In the 1960s, the porch succumbed to rot and decay, and was removed. When our clients bought the house, much-needed interior work kept the porch project on the back burner. But images of leisurely summer evenings dining on the porch overlooking the canal and listening to rockers creaking finally inspired them to rebuild the porch.

Rediscovering History

The only record of the original porch was a color snapshot, faded and dog-eared, that the owners had saved while waiting to rebuild the porch. It was difficult to make out all the original detailing from the photograph, but we could see the flat roof as well as the gentle arches curving sweetly across each bay.

In addition to the photo, we found further clues on the existing exterior walls of the house. The brick was corbeled out to create a drip edge, a detail that gave us the finish-floor height. In addition, vacant girder pockets that once held the porch floor and ceiling joists sat like pockmarks in the brick wall. In the ground, remnants of piers indicated the porch dimensions and the column rhythms, and the long black line that scarred the brick wall beneath the second-floor windows indicated where the porch roof had been sealed to the house with tar.

Porch Becomes a Veranda

Armed with these details, our crew here at Princeton Design Guild began to redesign the porch to create a generous, comforting edge to the severe-looking three-story brick wall. More than just porch, we designed a veranda that was 8 ft. deep and more than 160 ft. long.

The dining room, living room, family room, and kitchen all open onto the veranda from three sides of the house. This new corridor around the perimeter of the house gives each of these spaces a generous new

These photos saved by the owner were the only record of the porch. The top photo reveals the graceful arches, but also the flat roof that caused the porch to fail. The bottom photo shows the empty girder pockets and the tar line of the old roof.

anteroom to the exterior world, creating new and flexible traffic routes to and from the outside.

The west side of the porch, which faces the canal, is great for afternoon rocking in the setting sun. The southwest corner, where the house jogs back, creates an open outdoor dining area. A wide, welcoming staircase leads to a formal entrance on the north side, while the east side provides a private play area for the kids.

Piers Made of Chimney Block

We started by digging and pouring 22 footings. Piers that support the porch were built on top of the footings and tied into the rebar cast into each footing. Because the porch columns above the floor had to line up directly over the piers, we had to be extremely precise when locating the piers.

Each pier was built of 16-in. chimney block. As we stacked the block, we tied together four columns of rebar that thread up the center cavity (where the flue would normally have been). We then filled the core of each pier with concrete.

At the top of each pier, we added a block to the front face, which allowed us to hide the double 2x10 treated girders that span from each pier to the girder pockets in the brick wall of the house. The pockets, which were made for nineteenth-century wood, had to be modified and recut to accommodate the wood of the 1990s. We then ran 2x8 treated floor joists parallel to the outside walls on top of the girders 16 in. o.c. The 1x4 tongue-and-groove mahogany flooring was installed directly on top of the joists.

We gave the girders a slight pitch (⅛ in. per ft.) away from the house wall. Although plans called for a full roof over the porch, I was concerned that blowing rain and snow could end up on the floor. Creating a pitch ensured that any water would drain away safely.

The flooring was run perpendicular to the house wall so that water runs off parallel to the seams, not across them. We sealed the floor and let it cure for two days before setting the twenty 6x6 treated posts that form the core of each column. Each post is screwed to a base bolted into solid blocking below. We braced the posts plumb and then connected them with a box beam. T-straps strengthen the intersection of post and beam.

A Structural Slice through the Veranda

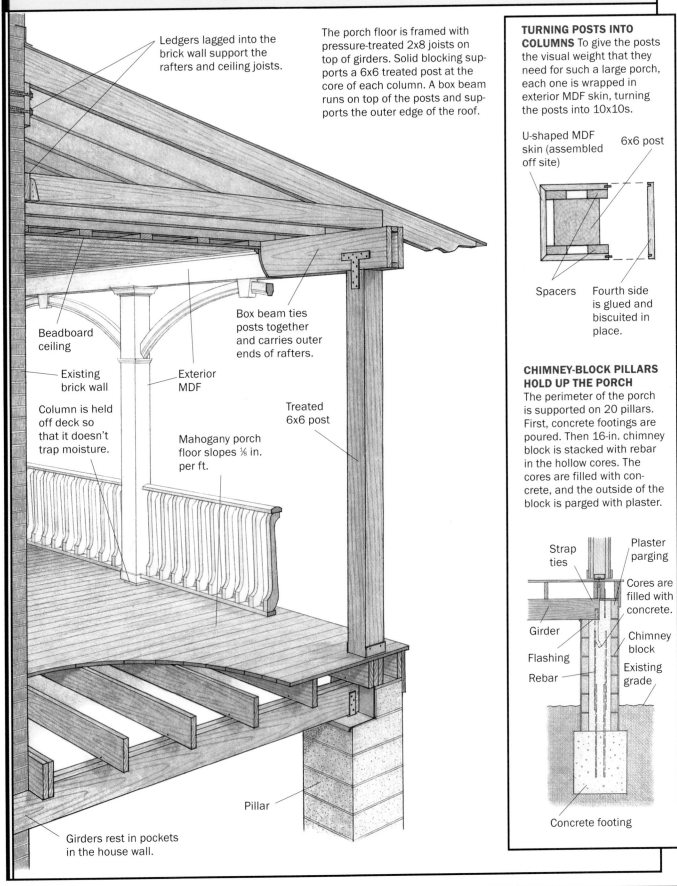

Ledgers lagged into the brick wall support the rafters and ceiling joists.

The porch floor is framed with pressure-treated 2x8 joists on top of girders. Solid blocking supports a 6x6 treated post at the core of each column. A box beam runs on top of the posts and supports the outer edge of the roof.

Beadboard ceiling

Existing brick wall

Column is held off deck so that it doesn't trap moisture.

Exterior MDF

Box beam ties posts together and carries outer ends of rafters.

Treated 6x6 post

Mahogany porch floor slopes ⅛ in. per ft.

Pillar

Girders rest in pockets in the house wall.

TURNING POSTS INTO COLUMNS To give the posts the visual weight that they need for such a large porch, each one is wrapped in exterior MDF skin, turning the posts into 10x10s.

U-shaped MDF skin (assembled off site)

6x6 post

Spacers

Fourth side is glued and biscuited in place.

CHIMNEY-BLOCK PILLARS HOLD UP THE PORCH
The perimeter of the porch is supported on 20 pillars. First, concrete footings are poured. Then 16-in. chimney block is stacked with rebar in the hollow cores. The cores are filled with concrete, and the outside of the block is parged with plaster.

Strap ties

Plaster parging

Cores are filled with concrete.

Girder

Flashing

Chimney block

Rebar

Existing grade

Concrete footing

The porch provides access to rooms inside the house while creating a spot for a leisurely swing in the hammock on a sunny afternoon.

These posts and box beams set the basic supporting structure of the porch roof.

New Roof with a Pitch

The roof was the final structural part of the porch to build. I suspect that problems with the flat roof over the original porch led to its demise. In the new design, we changed the roof to a 3-in-12 shed roof that would drain water easily. On the house side, the rafters were installed on a ledger epoxy-bolted to the brick wall, with the box beam supporting the other ends of the rafters. We extended the eaves to a depth of 3 ft. to allow better rain protection for the tops of the columns and to emphasize the ornamental aspect of the roof edge. Each rafter terminates in an S-curve that tapers to a wedge. This shape echoes the wooden brackets on the gables of the main house.

The roof sheathing went on quickly, and we covered the lower edge with ice-shield membrane and 30-lb. felt paper the rest of the way up. The roof was finished with three-tab asphalt shingles. We sealed the new roof to the building by scoring the brick around the perimeter and inserting copper counterflashing. A beadboard ceiling finished off the roof from below.

Adding the Dressing

With the porch structure basically complete, we turned our attention to the columns, arches, and railings. We didn't want the new porch to suffer the same fate as the old, so each 6x6 post was wrapped with ¾-in. exterior medium-density fiberboard (MDF) that would be the first line of defense against rot (top right drawing, p. 21). This MDF skin also turned the posts into 10x10 columns that had the visual weight and heft needed for this size porch.

We built the MDF columns in our shop, assembling three sides in a U-shape that was then slipped around the posts. The final face was biscuited and glued in place to complete the columns. The MDF was sealed on both sides and was held slightly off the porch floor to stop moisture from being trapped.

The tops and bottoms of the columns were finished off with mahogany moldings. Next, we installed the prefabricated arches and keystones between the columns. The arches were made from three layers of mahogany laminated together. A computer-controlled router cut the decorative profiles in each arch. The keystones, which are solely decorative, were made in two halves that lock over and around the top of each arch.

The porch railings were part custom, part stock. We purchased S-shaped Victorian clear-cedar balusters from a nearby railing-parts company. We designed our own railing cap, a wide, gently curved mahogany piece with stepped edges. The railing sheds water but doesn't offer a place for people to put cups.

We used the same railing detail on all three sets of stairs. On each set of stairs, we installed an additional pipe handrail that follows the wood railing, making the stairs code-compliant and easier to climb.

Kevin Wilkes is the founder of Princeton Design Guild, a design/build firm in Princeton, New Jersey.

A Screened-Porch Addition

■ BY JERRY GERMER

Screened porches have graced our homes since horse tails were first woven into screens in the mid-1800s. On hot summer evenings, people would sit on the porch, perhaps in a swing hung from the roof, and pass the time with family, friends, and neighbors. But in the middle of the twentieth century, when postwar builders were faced with the need to build massive numbers of houses quickly and economically,

they built smaller houses on smaller lots. Large outside porches no longer fit the houses or the lots. Lifestyles changed, too: People were spending more of their free time inside and in front of the television.

Recently, however, screened porches have been making a quiet comeback. Has television lost its charm or are people rediscovering the outdoors? I'm not sure, but for our family, a screened porch was the only way

To avoid having to close off the space under the porch, the author cantilevered the structure over a small bank into the backyard.

we could enjoy the beauty of our rural New Hampshire site without being assaulted by hordes of pesky insects.

Making Plans

The north side of the house off the living room seemed the obvious location for the new porch. Snugged against the house on its shadiest and most private side, the porch could project over the small bank that drops away to the backyard. A 3-ft.-wide walkway could run along the back wall of the house, connecting the porch with the back door near the kitchen. That way, we'd be able to bring food out onto the porch without having to negotiate steps or pass through the living room. Steps would lead from just outside the porch deck to the lawn.

To economize on materials, I decided to lay out the plan on a 3-ft. by 3-ft. grid, yielding a 15-ft. by 9-ft. deck floor—just about right for barbecue equipment, a small table and a few chairs. An existing window and the wall section below it would be cut out of the living room wall to provide a passageway to the porch from indoors. A screen door would link the porch to the stairs and to the deck/walkway.

Getting the Deck to Float

The bank at the rear of the house drops off about 5 ft. right away. If I built the new porch at the same level as the living-room floor, the open space below the porch would range from 1 ft. to 4 ft. Closing off this space with open, lattice-type skirting would have been tricky, and a solid foundation seemed an even less attractive alternative—I didn't want to stand in the backyard and see a 4-ft. high wall of parged concrete block.

A simpler and more elegant solution was to cantilever the floor structure over the sloping bank, supporting the joists on a perpendicular 4x10 beam 6 ft. from the house. The beam rests atop two 4x4 posts, which bear on

Section through Porch

PVC gutter

FRP panels

2x4 purlin

2x8 rafter

3-piece fascia

Fiberglass screen stapled to 2x4 posts and covered with 1x2 strips

2x4s

2x8 floor joist

4x4 post

Fiberglass screen stapled over joists

4-in. x 10-in. beam

If ever I have occasion to build another screened porch, I'll take the time to come up with a solution that allows for periodic cleaning of the floor screen.

concrete footings resting about 3 ft. below grade. The posts are spaced 9 ft. apart, so the beam cantilevers out 3 ft. at each end. I used 2x8s on 3-ft. centers for floor joists, fastening one end of each joist (with a joist hanger) to a 2x8 ledger bolted to the house sill.

The floor of the porch consists of 2x4 boards in continuous lengths, spaced ½ in. apart and screwed to the joists. All structural members, as well as the decking, are pressure-treated southern yellow pine. The effect, with the house's skirtboard wrapping around the joists is of a porch that floats out over the bank.

With no foundation walls to which I could attach screen, though, I needed to find another way of maintaining continuity of the insect barrier. The only solution that came to mind was to screen the floor. That's why I stapled fiberglass screen over the tops of the joists, before screwing down the decking. It worked; bugs can't get up through the bottom of the deck. But after two years of summertime use, the porch revealed the flaw in my scheme. Bits of debris, ranging from dust to pencils, fall into the cracks and get trapped by the screen. Vacuuming has been only partially effective in cleaning out the cracks, but then again, our aging Electrolux® no longer has the suck it once did. Nevertheless, if ever I have occasion to build another screened porch, I'll take the time to come up with a solution that allows for periodic cleaning of the floor screen.

Daylight and Privacy

I wanted the walls of the porch to be as light and open as possible, yet still offer some privacy. Because the roof structure would be very lightweight, supporting posts were kept lean as well—2x4s on 3-ft. centers. Two posts meet at the corners so that neither post overlaps the inside face of the other. I stapled 36-in. widths of black fiberglass insect screen to the inside face of each post,

A three-tiered 15-in. fascia conceals a very shallow-pitched shed roof constructed of pressure-treated framing and corrugated, fiber-reinforced plastic (FRP) panels.

and then secured 1x2 wood strips over the stapled edges with drywall screws.

Black screen over regularly spaced posts doesn't make for a very interesting wall surface, however, nor does it provide much in the way of privacy. Hoping to take care of both of these problems, I wrapped 30-in. high panels of 1x2 balusters around three sides of the porch. The panels are screwed to the outside faces of the posts, which allows removal of the panels for maintenance and repainting. The effect though, with all balusters spaced approximately on 5-in. centers, is of a continuous rail.

Keeping Rain out, Letting Light In

Most roofed porches have a downside. In providing a sheltered space outdoors, they shade the windows, darkening the rooms. While summers here are short, winters are long, and gray days abound. When I remodeled our house, I tried to maximize passive-solar gain. By adding more windows on the south side of the house and removing non-bearing interior partitions on the first floor, I'd been able both to warm the house and to make it feel lighter and more cheerful. But in my zeal for energy efficiency, I had also eliminated some north-facing windows. I didn't want to block the remaining light from the north windows by shading them with an opaque porch roof.

"Why not design a roof that would allow light to pass through?" I thought to myself. If I could find the right material, the idea might have promise. Glass was ruled out immediately as being too expensive. Options in plastic included double-skinned polycarbonate sheet (such as Exolite®) and corrugated fiber-reinforced plastic (FRP). Exolite would work but isn't cheap. FRP would be cheap, but to drain properly, the panels would have to overhang the eaves. The exposed ends, undulating like a washboard, would fit better on a shed or a chicken coop—not at all in keeping with the character of our house. If I were to use the FRP, I would have to come up with an eave detail that hid the corrugated panel ends without impeding drainage.

A Shallow Pitch Concealed

The two challenges were how to make the porch roof seem to belong to the house and how to hide the corrugated ends of the FRP from view. A shed roof that matched the pitch of the house's roof would run into the second-floor windows. And a shallower pitched roof would seem an afterthought. A completely level roof, on the other hand, would underscore the house's horizontal eaves and frieze board. But I still needed to provide some slope for drainage. A solution was suggested by the roofing material itself.

Because the panels are 12 ft. long, I'd be able to use them full length (no horizontal lap joints), all but eliminating the chance of wind-driven rain getting up under my roofing. I figured I could get by with a minimum pitch for drainage—¼ in. per ft. Later, I could wrap a fascia around the three exposed sides of the roof to hide the rafters, getting a flat-looking roof with good drainage.

Because my goal was to let in as much light as possible, I left all roof framing exposed. The 2x8 rafters, spaced 3 ft. o.c., run perpendicular to the house, dropping 3 in. in 12 ft. The high ends of the rafters are fastened to a 2x8 ledger lag-bolted to the house. The lower ends of the rafters extend 15 in. past the top of the outer wall, to carry the fascia. I also ran 2x4 purlins (22 in. o.c.) 15 in. out to support the fascia at the side walls. Two ⅛ in. cables run diagonally under the rafters, corner to corner, to brace the roof against racking. The FRP panels were then attached to the purlins with aluminum roofing nails and rubber washers. The nails are spaced 6 in. to 8 in. o.c. (I had to predrill the panels).

Details, Details

Concealing the rafters and the FRP would require a 15-in.-wide fascia, which I felt would

Vertical cleats nailed to the joist support the fascia. Flashing and an angled 1x6 protect the fascia boards from runoff.

be too heavy-looking if installed in one piece. Some horizontal lines would be necessary to reduce the apparent width of the fascia and to add a little interest to an otherwise plain facade. So I built a three-level fascia, with layered boards of diminishing size.

Behind the fascia, the FRP panels project over the porch's front wall by about 1 in. A PVC gutter attached to an interior fascia above the screen wall collects runoff and carries it to downspout tees at each end. Rather than run downspouts down the corners of the porch, where they would have messed up the corner-post detail, I elected to let the water drip directly to the ground.

The translucent roof panels function well in winter, allowing a great deal of northern light into the house. In the summer, the porch is shaded by the house throughout the day, except for early in the morning and late in the afternoon, which was a nuisance. To resolve the problem simply and inexpensively, I draped sheets of burlap on 1x1 battens from eyehooks screwed into the purlins, a solution that has worked quite nicely.

Jerry Germer is an architect and writer living in Marlborough, New Hampshire.

A Builder's Screen Porch

■ BY SCOTT MCBRIDE

The screen porch the author built on his own house combines Victorian detailing with a builder's considered construction methods.

My grandfather lived alone in a little bungalow by the seashore. We got to know each other in his final years by spending long summer evenings out on the screen porch. We talked about the many things the old man had done in his life and some of the things a young man might do with his. Sometimes we didn't talk at all—just listened to the waves and the pinging of the June bugs off the screen, watched the lights, smelled the breeze.

A screen porch at night can have a magic all its own, balancing as it does on the cusp between interior and exterior space. A porch offers just enough protection from the elements to foster relaxation and reflection, without shutting out the sounds and the smells of the cosmos. This dual nature of screen porches can make them difficult to build with style because the usual rules of interior and exterior construction often overlap in their design.

When the time came to build a screen porch on my own house here in Virginia, I had the luxury of time—no anxious client, no deadline, and no hourly wages to worry about. So I included lots of special details that I hope will spare my porch some of the problems I've seen in 20 years of remodeling other people's houses.

The Foundation

I sited my screen porch two risers up from grade and three risers down from the adjacent kitchen. This made a smooth transition to the yard without requiring too much of a descent when carrying an armful of dinner plates from the kitchen. To anchor the structure visually, I ran a continuous step of pressure-treated lumber around the perimeter as a sort of plinth.

The step is supported by pressure-treated lookouts that cantilever off a poured-concrete foundation. I used pressure-treated 2x8s for the lookouts, inserted them into my formwork, and actually poured the concrete around and over them. There isn't much concrete above the lookouts, so to key each lookout into the mix, I nailed a joist hanger on both sides. A week after the pour, the projecting lookouts were rock solid.

A Hip-Framed Floor

Masonry is the obvious choice for the floor of a screen porch because water blowing through the screens won't affect it. Also, in hot weather the coolness of a masonry floor feels good on your bare feet. On the downside, masonry is, well, hard. It's also difficult to keep clean, it's gritty underfoot, and it retains moisture in damp weather.

Open decking is a good alternative to masonry, as long as it's screened underneath to keep the bugs out. Spaced, pressure-treated yellow pine will make a good, serviceable floor, and having a roof overhead will protect the floor from the harsh sun, which is the nemesis of pressure-treated lumber. But open decking looks utilitarian at best, and

A single pressure-treated step runs all the way around the outside of the porch as a sort of plinth.

Lookouts embedded in the concrete (and held securely by the addition of a joist hanger nailed to each side) provide rock-solid support for the first tread of the step that runs around the porch's perimeter.

my wife and I wanted something a bit more refined.

I decided to use untreated kiln-dried yellow-pine flooring, bordered by a coping of treated 2x8 (right photo, p. 30). I have repaired a lot of old porches, and I have noticed that it's the outer ends of the old floors

This floor system, which is framed like a shallow hip roof, allows water to run off the porch floor. Strapped joists bring the finish floor flush with the 2x8 coping.

A coping of pressure-treated 2x8s supports the porch posts. Weep channels in the coping and an aluminum pan divert rainwater blown through the screens.

Open decking is a good alternative to masonry, as long as it's screened underneath to keep the bugs out.

that eventually decay while the wood stays sound just a foot or so in from the drip line of the eaves. By bordering my floor with a treated coping, the untreated yellow-pine flooring would be recessed farther under cover. Also, the coping would allow me to lay the tongue-and-groove (T&G) floor at the end of the job because the structure above—the roof and its supporting columns—bears on the coping, not on the flooring. A temporary plywood floor endured weather and foot traffic during construction and allowed me easy access to run wires in the 1-ft.-deep crawl space.

To ensure positive drainage and to avoid standing water on the T&G floor, I pitched the floor, ¼ in. per foot from its center in three directions. This meant that I'd have to frame the floor like a shallow hip roof (photo, above left). What became the ridge of the floor framing was supported by concrete piers.

I ran 1x strapping perpendicular to the joists and eventually laid the flooring over the strapping. In addition to promoting good air circulation under the flooring, the strapping served two other purposes: It allowed the flooring to run parallel to the slope so that most of the water would flow by the joints in the flooring rather than into them. The strapping also brings the top of the 1x flooring flush with the 2x coping. I could have used pressure-treated 1x for the

coping, but because the roof and its supporting posts rest on the coping, I wanted it to be substantial.

The joint between the ends of the flooring and the inside edge of the coping gave me pause. I knew that wind-driven water was likely to seep in here and be sucked up by the end grain of the flooring, leading to decay. I thought about leaving the joint intentionally open, say ¼ in., but I knew that such a gap would collect dirt and be an avenue for critters. Instead, I back-cut the ends of the floorboards at a 45° angle and let them cantilever a couple of inches past the strapping for good air circulation underneath. Meanwhile, the long point of the mitered end butts tightly to the coping.

To collect any water that might seep through the joint, I formed aluminum pans that run underneath the coping and lip out over the floor framing (photo, above right). I cut weep channels in the underside of the coping with a dado head mounted on my radial-arm saw to let water out and air in. I have since heard that aluminum reacts with the copper in treated wood, so I probably should have used copper for the pans.

Hollow Posts and Beams

The roof of a screen porch is generally supported by posts and beams rather than by walls. Solid pressure-treated posts work well for support, but they won't accommodate wiring or light switches. Solid posts also are prone to shrinking, twisting, and checking.

I made hollow posts of clear fir, joining them with resorcinol glue. Biscuits provided registration during glue up (middle drawing, right). I rabbeted the sides of the posts to receive both the frames for the screen panels and the solid panels below the screens. The bottom of each post was rabbeted to house cast-aluminum post pedestals. The pedestals keep the bottoms of the posts dry. They also allow air to circulate inside the posts to dry up any internal condensation. Rabbeting the pedestals into the posts makes them almost invisible and ensures that all rainwater is carried safely down past the joint between the pedestal and the post.

Because the 2x8 coping on which the pedestals bear is pitched (owing to the hipped floor framing), I used a stationary belt sander to grind the feet of the pedestals to match.

Inland Virginia where I live doesn't get the wind of the Florida coast, but we get plenty of gales, and last year a tornado ripped the roof off a Wal-Mart™ in another part of the state. To provide uplift resistance for my porch roof, I bolted the tops and bottoms of the posts in place. Rather than relying on weak end grain to hold the bolts, I ran horizontal pairs of steel dowels through the posts, 3½ in. from the top and the bottom (top and bottom drawings, right). The dowels were hacksawed from ⅜-in.-dia. spikes. At the bottom, I passed a lag bolt vertically between the dowels and screwed it down into the floor framing until the head of the lag came to bear against the dowels (bottom drawing, right). At the top, I used a similar arrangement, but instead of lag bolts, I used inverted J-bolts with the foot of the J mortised into the top of the rough beam and the threaded end passing between the dowels. To get at the bolts with a wrench, I cut slots on the interior sides of the posts, which would be covered later with base and capital

Porch Posts: Construction and Attachment Details

To prevent uplift from strong winds, the hollow posts are bolted at the bottom to the 2x8 coping and at the top to the rough beam.

TOP OF POST

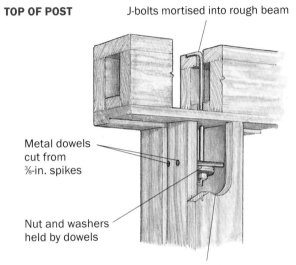

J-bolts mortised into rough beam

Metal dowels cut from ⅜-in. spikes

Nut and washers held by dowels

Slots cut in top and bottom of posts for wrench access

MIDDLE OF POST

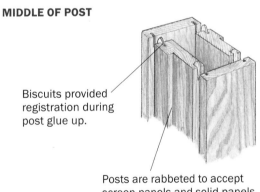

Biscuits provided registration during post glue up.

Posts are rabbeted to accept screen panels and solid panels.

BOTTOM OF POST

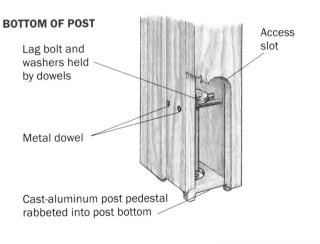

Access slot

Lag bolt and washers held by dowels

Metal dowel

Cast-aluminum post pedestal rabbeted into post bottom

Primary and secondary rafters combined with a series of purlins make up the porch's roof system. The secondary rafters curve along their bottom edges to reduce their width from 9 in. to 5 in. The purlins are let into the rafters and secured with screws.

To create the curves on the bottom edge of the secondary rafters, the author first rough cut the edges with a jigsaw, then trimmed them using a template and a router fitted with a flush-trimming bit.

trim. I was surprised how rigid the posts felt after being bolted upright, even before they were tied together at the top.

The rough beams were made up with a box cross section rather than simply doubling up 2xs on edge (drawing, facing page). This gave the beam lateral as well as vertical strength so that any unresolved thrust loads from the untrussed secondary rafters above would be resisted by the horizontal top plate in the beam.

The Roof and the Ceiling

The inspiration for the coffered cathedral ceiling came from several sources. I once watched Japanese carpenters raise the frame of a small farmhouse. The delicate grid of the peeled white timbers against the sky made a lasting impression. I've also worked on Victorian houses in the Hudson Valley that featured finely wrought coffered ceilings over their verandas.

The framing scheme I finally decided on is one that's found in some New England timber frames: trussed pairs of principle rafters interspersed with lighter, untrussed secondary rafters.

Instead of using heavy timber, I laminated each principle rafter in place from a 2x6 sandwiched between two 2x10s. Offsetting the bottom edge of the 2x6 helped disguise the joints, and the hollow channel above the 2x6 was useful for wiring.

Collar ties connecting principle rafter pairs have a 2x6 core sandwiched between 1x8s. The ¾-in. thickness of the 1x8 avoids an undesirable flush joint at the end where it butts into the rafter.

The secondary rafters are as wide as the principle rafters at the base, but their lower edges immediately arch up into a curve that reduces their width from 9 in. to 5 in. The constant width of all the rafters at the base allows the bird's mouth and frieze-block conditions to be uniform, even though the rafter width varies. I roughed out the curve of the secondary rafters with a jigsaw, then trimmed them with a flush-trimming router bit guided by a template.

Short 2x4 purlins span between the rafters on approximately 2-ft. centers. The ends of the purlins are housed in shallow pockets routed into the rafters, also with the help of a plywood template. I fastened the purlins with long galvanized screws.

The roof-framing material was selected from common yellow-pine framing lumber.

Floor Framing and Post Details

The porch is supported by a series of hollow posts. Plywood wain-scot panels provide lateral rigidity. The wainscot panels and the shop-made screen panels fit into the rabbets cut into the posts.

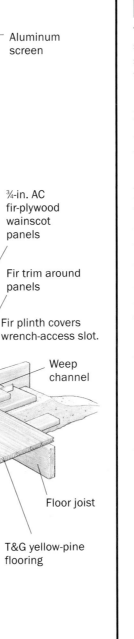

Box-section rough beams

Shop-made screen panels

Fir capital covers wrench-access slot.

Aluminum screen

Hollow post accommodates wiring.

¾-in. AC fir-plywood wainscot panels

¼-in. lauan plywood

Fir trim around panels

2x8 pressure-treated coping

Fir plinth covers wrench-access slot.

Aluminum pan

Continuous step around porch perimeter

Weep channel

Joist hanger

Floor joist

1x strapping

T&G yellow-pine flooring

Pressure-treated lookout embedded in concrete

The author used a chicken ladder—a narrow set of stairs built on site—to ease the task of installing the vertical sheathing that runs from the eaves to the ridge.

Before I remilled the lumber, I stickered it and covered it with plywood for two months to let it dry.

The roof was sheathed with 2x6 T&G yellow pine run vertically, perpendicular to the purlins. The exposed V-joint side faces down, and the flush side faces up. Running the boards vertically added to the illusion of the porch's interior height; it was difficult to install because I had to maneuver from the eaves to the ridge while nailing each piece. To facilitate the process, I built a chicken ladder—a narrow staircase that hooks over the ridge and runs down to the eaves.

Building a structure with an exposed finished frame was difficult and time-consuming. Floor space in my shop was strained to the max while all the components were fabricated. Everything had to be given multiple coats of a water-repellent finish to prepare it for the eventuality of rain before I could dry in the structure—I used Olympic® WaterGuard® from PPG Industries®. Moving ladders and scaffolding around all that finished woodwork was harrowing. The payoff, though, was a structure with a kind of bare-bones integrity that would have been hard to achieve with the conventional approach of rough framing wrapped with finish material.

Yellow pine and Douglas fir complement one another on the interior of the porch. The rafter system, the vertical roof sheathing, and the flooring are all yellow pine while the posts and the panels are Douglas fir.

The structure itself gains much-needed shear strength from the wainscoting below each screen panel.

Finish Details

To contrast with the yellow pine in the ceiling and the floor, I used fir for all the woodwork from the floor up to the interior frieze. The choice of fir allowed me to order matching stock screen doors, and this saved a lot of time in the shop. To reinforce the doors against racking, I introduced slender diagonal compression braces into the doors' lower screen panels.

The structure itself gains much-needed shear strength from the wainscoting below each screen panel. The wainscoting has no interior framing: It is built up with plywood and trim boards. First I screwed ¾-in. AC fir plywood panels to the posts, good side in. I bedded the panels into the same rabbets that would receive the screen frames above the wainscoting. I then attached 5/4 fir rails

and stiles to the inside face of the fir plywood. To avoid exposed nail heads, I screwed through the back of the panel to catch the trim.

On the outside, I tacked a sheet of ¼-in. lauan over the back of the AC plywood. Lauan holds up well in exterior applications and takes a good paint finish. The stiles and the rails on the outside were nailed through both layers of plywood into the interior stiles and rails. The resulting sandwich proved remarkably stiff. I capped the panels with a beveled sill and a rabbeted stool.

For drainage, the bottom edge of the wainscoting was raised 1 in. above the floor coping. To keep bugs out, I stapled a narrow skirt of insect screen around the outside. The top of this skirt was clamped down with a thin wooden band. A similar condition was achieved at the doors by attaching sweeps of insect screen. I even weather-stripped the edges of screen doors using a compressible-rubber weatherstripping.

When it came time to lay the T&G floor, I pondered the best way to deal with the shallow hips where the pitch of the floor changes direction. Rather than have a continuous 45° joint, which would be prone to opening up and collecting dirt, I decided to weave the floorboards in a herringbone pattern. Working from the longest boards out to the shortest, I grooved the end of each board so that it would engage the leading tongued edge of its neighbor. To cut the end groove, I used a ¼-in. wing cutter chucked in a router. The result is a pleasing stepped pattern that is accentuated by the way sunlight bounces off the wood according to the grain direction and the different planes of the hipped floor. Depending on where you stand, the floor has almost a faceted look; one side of the hip looks darker than the other.

Outside, I finished the porch with details consistent with my late-nineteenth-century house. I extended the cornice return all the way across the gable by cantilevering lookouts off the gable studding. This creates a full pediment and gives the porch's gable end the same overhang protection as its eaves. The tops of the posts sport scroll brackets on the outside and simple capitals on the inside.

Screen for the Porch

I made wood frames for my porch screens out of 1x2 fir. I used mortise-and-tenon joinery with an offset shoulder on the rails. The strength of a mortise-and-tenon joint isn't really necessary for a fixed frame that gets fully supported in a larger structure. But the design of this joint makes it easy to use a table saw to cut the rabbets and plow the spline grooves before assembling the frame.

Spline stock holds the screen in the frame. Tubular in cross section, the spline stock gets pushed into a groove on the frame where its compression holds the screen in place. Spline stock is made from rubber or vinyl, and it's available in a smooth profile or with ridges around the circumference. The ridges help guide the splining tool, and they give the spline a little more bite on the walls of the groove.

The tool used to press in the spline looks like a double-ended pizza cutter. One disk has a convex edge used initially to crease the screen into the groove. The other disk has a concave edge, which tracks on the round spline as it is pressed into the groove.

The two most common types of screen are aluminum and vinyl. Aluminum screen is available in mill finish or charcoal.

I used mill-finish aluminum for my screen porch because it seemed to be the most transparent. I also think aluminum is somewhat stronger than vinyl and less likely to sag over wide spans. The main drawback of aluminum is oxidation, which gradually forms a grainy deposit on the wire and reduces the screen's transparency. I live in a rural inland area where salt and pollution aren't prevalent. If I lived near the sea or in an urban environment, I would have leaned toward vinyl. I would also go with vinyl if I were hanging the screen in place vertically,

The hipped floor slopes in three directions to shed water that blows through the screens. Sun hitting the finished floor gives a pleasing effect. The joists are cross-strapped, and the flooring is laid on the strapping so that it runs parallel to the slope of the porch floor.

A router grooved the end of each piece of flooring so that it could herringbone its way down the floor's hips.

rather than rolling it out on a bench. Vinyl is much easier to work with and less likely to crease. A final consideration in choosing screen is the resounding ping made by bugs slamming into a tightly stretched aluminum screen. I rather enjoy it—it's one of the unique sounds of summer—but others might prefer to muffle the impact by using the softer vinyl screen.

Scott McBride is a contributing editor of Fine Homebuilding *and the author of* Build Like a Pro™: Windows and Doors, *published by The Taunton Press.*

A Screen Porch Dresses Up a Ranch

■ BY ALEX L. VARGA

"Something there is that doesn't love a wall; that wants it down." I know these lines from Robert Frost's "Mending Wall" evoke a deeper meaning; however, it seems that this sentiment applies whenever humans endeavor to build a sound and lasting structure. There is always some element of nature or turn of fashion that conspires to alter the structure once it is completed.

I wonder what Frost would have written had he been building a wooden structure. I know I had my work cut out for me when I added a screen porch to a ranch house in Connecticut. My clients requested a shaded outdoor living area that provided views and took advantage of cool breezes coming from the wooded area behind their house. The catch was that the outdoor living area should have a finished wood floor and lots of wood trim. Digging the foundation 42 in. below grade to get under the frost line was only part of the solution. Here I'll discuss how I designed and built a porch to survive the elements as it provides a beautiful refuge from summer heat and pesky bugs.

The porch includes a stone patio and an octagonal, covered entry. These elements don't just look good, they help keep water away from the porch. In addition, the porch's roof features large overhangs and gutters for protection from sun and rain.

Cypress Frame over Crushed Stone

When planning the porch, I followed basic moisture-control strategies: allowing for drainage, creating ventilation, and keeping wood out of direct contact with the ground. During the beginning stages of the project, work was required on the house's septic system. With the backhoe on site, I took the opportunity to cut the grade down about 2 ft. in the porch area. I also sloped the grade away from the house.

With the backhoe I then dug six 42-in.-deep holes for the concrete foundation piers. Once the piers were in place, I bolted triple 2x10 beams around the perimeter of the porch, supported by the piers and bolted securely to them.

Taking the grade down 2 ft. allowed me to add a layer of crushed stone about 3 in. deep and still have almost a foot of clearance beneath the porch's floor joists. The crushed stone creates a clean and well-drained area under the floor.

The floor joists are 2x8 cypress, which costs a bit more than pressure-treated pine but is naturally, as opposed to chemically, rot resistant. Spaced on 2-ft. centers, the joists are connected with joist hangers to the perimeter beams and to a triple 2x10 center-span beam.

To prevent small animals from getting under the floor system, I attached galvanized-steel wire mesh to the inside surface of the perimeter beams, bent the wire back about 6 in. along the ground and covered the wire with crushed stone. During this phase of construction, I also prepared the site for a stone patio. The patio encircles the porch and extends slightly beneath it; the floor framing is about 3 in. above the perimeter stonework. Unlike the soil and plants that often surround porches, the stone patio allows rainwater to drain away from the porch, giving it a better shot at staying dry

and ventilated. The patio also looks great and helps unify the new construction and the existing house.

Another basic moisture-control measure I took was to provide air circulation underneath the porch. I faced the perimeter beams with a cedar skirtboard that's ¾ in. above the stone. This ¾-in. gap runs continuously around the porch and lets air flow freely through the floor system.

Continuous Headers and Braced Posts Make for Open Walls

After putting single 2x4 pilasters at the house and double 2x4 posts at the corners of the floor frame, I installed two 24-ft.-long 6x8 header beams on top of the pilasters and posts. The header beams run continuously from the house out to their free ends, which cantilever 2 ft. 6 in. beyond the free-standing posts that rest on the stone patio.

I wanted to keep the sidewalls of the porch open to catch summer breezes and to capture the view of the woods as clearly as I could. So I used single 2x4 posts on 5-ft. centers, which would later be fully cased in 1x trim, to frame the screen openings. Single 2x4 blocks at chair-rail height stabilize the posts against bending and twisting and make the finished screen sizes large but manageable.

The continuous 6x8 headers solidly connect the individual posts together at their tops and create a stable and rigid frame out of a row of rather slender posts. The casing of the posts in 1x trim and the horizontal bracing provided by the chair-rail blocks allow the single 2x4 posts to bear the necessary roof loads easily. To add to the rigidity of these sidewall frames, I used sections of 3-in. steel angle with 8d nails to connect the corner posts to the floor system and to the header beams. These angle brackets were later hidden underneath the finish trim work.

Section of Porch Wall at Floor

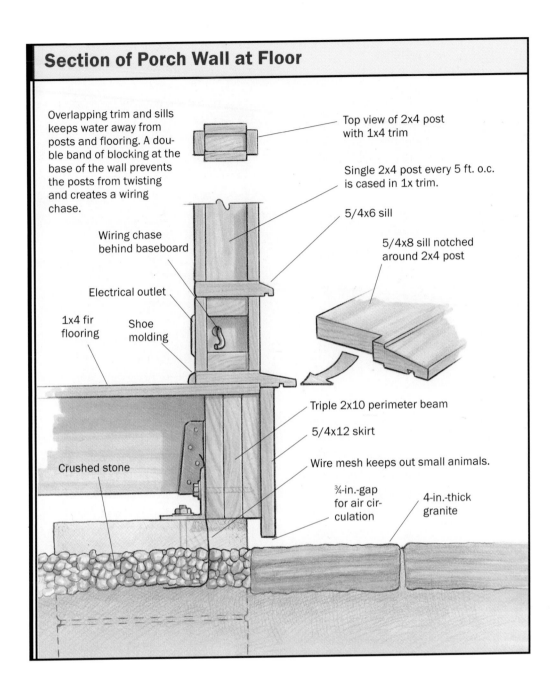

Overlapping trim and sills keeps water away from posts and flooring. A double band of blocking at the base of the wall prevents the posts from twisting and creates a wiring chase.

Wiring chase behind baseboard

Electrical outlet

1x4 fir flooring

Shoe molding

Crushed stone

Top view of 2x4 post with 1x4 trim

Single 2x4 post every 5 ft. o.c. is cased in 1x trim.

5/4x6 sill

5/4x8 sill notched around 2x4 post

Triple 2x10 perimeter beam

5/4x12 skirt

Wire mesh keeps out small animals.

¾-in.-gap for air circulation

4-in.-thick granite

I could have used a bottom plate, but instead I opted to install the 2x4 posts directly on the perimeter beams (drawing, above). I laid the flooring on the beams and capped the end grain with a 5/4x8 sill that's notched around the 2x4 posts. A double band of blocking topped with a 5/4x6 sill creates a wiring chase that, when covered with 1x4 trim, provides an attractive baseboard detail.

Site-Built Trusses Create a Branchlike Effect

Inside the porch, I wanted the roof structure to appear light and open, almost treelike in its framework. My idea was to link the structure to the lacework of the woods that the porch overlooks. So I designed a cathedral ceiling that would be supported by trusses

A scaffold provides a work station for assembling trusses on site. Heavy 6x8 beams spanning from the house to the porch's corner posts carry trusses constructed of 2x4s and custom-made steel plates. Heavy beams allow for open walls that are sheltered by 2-ft.-deep overhangs.

The porch roof overhangs the walls all around for shade and for rain protection.

built with small-dimension lumber, which evoked the image of tree branches better than a framework of rafters and collar ties.

I fabricated the trusses on site using 2x4 fir studs and ⅛-in. galvanized-steel plates cut with a jigsaw. After making patterns, I cut all the truss pieces on the ground and assembled the trusses in place, working from a scaffold (photo, above). The trusses are on 5-ft. centers.

Between the trusses, I installed doubled 2x4 rafters. The rafters are braced at the ridge and at midspan by 2x4 kickers nailed to the trusses. Fanning out from the trusses, the kickers provided the branchlike effect that I had been pursuing.

Installed with the bevel face down, the 2x6 tongue-and-groove roof boards provide a little texture, and the dark lines of the bevel joints look good with the 2x4 framework.

Overhangs Keep Porch Cool and Dry

The porch roof overhangs the walls all around for shade and for rain protection. At the eaves, 2-ft.-deep overhangs match the overhang depth on the existing house. The truss design allowed me to build these overhangs without using large collar ties. Such large members would have appeared much too heavy for the look I wanted. The trusses transfer all of the roof weight to the 6x8 headers, leaving the truss ends free to create the overhangs.

The large soffit overhangs also turned out to be a good place to locate floodlights to light the interior-ceiling surfaces. I hid these fixtures by adding a 1x6 trim detail to the inside top edge of the sidewall beams. Finished with exterior-grade fir plywood and painted to match the main house, the porch soffits are open to the interior. The gable end is also open, eliminating the need for any special soffit or ridge ventilation.

Curved Columns Resemble Tree Trunks

At the gable end, an 8-ft. overhang provides a covered section for sitting on the patio in addition to shading and keeping windblown rain from getting into the porch. This deep gable overhang rests on two curved columns I made in my shop. The columns are double 2x4s cased with primed and painted #2 cedar.

I got the curved look by gluing and nailing wedge-shaped blocks of 1x stock to the tops of the 2x4 cores. I ripped both edges of cedar casing so that it was tapered, then glued and nailed the casing to the cores. The bottom of a finished column is a 5-in. square; the top is an 8-in. square. The casing conforms to the posts, giving the columns a curving profile similar to that of a tree trunk.

Spacing the Roof Boards Creates a Skylight

As the roof structure was nearing completion, I realized that although the porch would be comfortably shady during the heat of summer, it might end up a bit too dark. So before installing the last several feet of 2x6 roof boards, I began experimenting with ideas for a ridge skylight. Rather than cut an opening or a series of openings into the roof deck, I decided to take a hint from the lines of the 2x6 roof boards. In the top 2 ft. on both sides of the peak, I separated the boards after ripping off the tongues on a table saw. Starting with a ¼-in. gap, I widened each joint between boards to 2 in. at the peak (photo, right).

Over these spaced roof boards I installed ⅜-in.-thick double-wall Lexan® sheets, which might be described as plastic, see-through cardboard. Lexan is obtainable from commercial-plastics distributors. First I folded each 4x8 sheet in half along its length, which was similar to folding a sheet of cardboard. Then I set the sheets in beads of silicone on top of the roof framing, leaving a ½-in. gap between the sheets for expansion. I then filled the gap with silicone.

I fastened the Lexan to the roof structure with battens made of ⅛-in. by 2-in. flat aluminum bar stock. I bent the aluminum to fit over the ridge, set the aluminum in silicone over the Lexan, and drilled pilot holes through the aluminum and the Lexan into the roof framing. Then I screwed the bar stock to the frame, locking the Lexan sky-

light in place. This simple but effective skylight allows enough light into the porch to brighten it without overheating it. The resulting light from the spaced 2x6 roof boards is similar to sunlight filtering through tree branches.

Trimmed Wall Posts Hold Site-Built Screens

For the trim on this project, I used a mix of cypress, red cedar, and white cedar that I primed on all sides with an oil-based primer. Cedar and cypress have natural resistance against rot and decay. All of the trim was finished with an acrylic latex paint to match the existing house finish.

With the framing trimmed out, I was left with a pattern of 5-ft.-square screen openings over smaller 5-ft. by 2-ft. screen openings. I

Because the roof has such deep overhangs, a ridge skylight was needed to brighten the porch. This unconventional skylight is a series of progressively wider gaps between roofing boards, all covered with a Lexan ridge cap. The trusses and 2x6 roof boards are finished with semitransparent stain similar to the gray of the floor and the stonework.

made all the screens using aluminum frame stock and aluminum screen. I made most of the screens on the ground and popped them into their openings. Then I held them in place with 1x2 stock set with finish nails. If a screen becomes damaged, the 1x2 is removed, and the screen comes right out.

In the upper section of the gable end, I had to fit screens into the triangular openings of a truss. I couldn't use manufactured square corner clips to join triangular frames; and the screen, which has a square cross mesh, wrinkled when I stretched it diagonally. I ended up screwing the frames in their openings and stretching the screen in place.

The southwest side of the porch is relatively exposed to both weather and neighbors. Here, I had a roll-down canvas storm shade installed to keep out windblown rain as well as the harsh southeast light in summer. The shade also is a privacy screen, blocking the porch's view from the neighbors' yard.

Tinted Marine Varnish Protects Strip Flooring

For the floor, I chose ¾-in. by 3½-in. tongue-and-groove (T&G) fir to achieve a smooth, attractive and easy-maintenance surface. The added advantage of T&G boards for the floor surface is that they create an insect barrier, eliminating the need for screening around the skirt or under the joists. There's no plywood. The flooring runs directly over the joists.

The flooring's color, however, was overly reddish next to the bluish gray of the granite patio. So I decided to mix a tinted but still transparent high-gloss finish. After some research and experimentation, I chose a marine-grade spar varnish as the primary sealing element because it's waterproof and UV resistant. I mixed the varnish with a small amount of bluish gray stain to help deaden the reddish tone of the fir. I applied four coats to the floor, resulting in a high-gloss, semitransparent finish with an attractive grayish tint. The only drawback I discovered to mixing the stain into the varnish was that it seemed to slow the curing process. The varnish remained fragile, even though it was dry to the touch, for about two weeks.

With open-air porches it is common practice to pitch the floor approximately ⅛ in. per ft. away from the main building to allow standing water to drain. With this porch, however, I chose not to pitch the floor so that I could keep all of my trim lines and screen openings level and parallel. I thought that the flooring's marine finish, the large roof overhangs with 4-in. aluminum gutters and the roll-down canvas storm screen would provide adequate protection to the interior from splashing water. This combination has proved itself effective.

As a second line of defense against water collecting on the porch floor, I installed ⅜-in. brass bushings on 5-ft. centers around the perimeter of the floor to serve as inconspicuous floor drains. These bushings function reasonably well; in the future, however, I probably will use a ¾-in. bushing to allow any intruding water to drain more easily.

Alex L. Varga is an architect in Hamden, Connecticut who specializes in custom home design.

Tinted marine varnish on the fir flooring and decay-resistant cedar and cypress trim, primed on all sides, allow for interior-quality details in the screen porch. In the soffit bays, 1x6 trim boards hide spotlights.

The seasonal porch keeps out afternoon sun in the summer and allows evening enjoyment of the deck. When cool weather arrives, the porch come down for a sunny southern exposure.

Adding a Seasonal Porch

■ BY KEN TEXTOR

In an age of maintenance-free building, a structure that requires attention at least twice a year may seem out of step. But as I look back, my decision to convert an open deck into a summers-only screened-in porch still makes sense to me.

From the outset, you must believe that it actually gets hot in Maine during the summer. We live in a small clearing in the woods, sheltered by tall, wind-shielding pines. On sunny days, the temperature on our open, south-facing deck regularly reaches well into the 90s, frequently topping 100° F or more.

Of course, by late afternoon it usually cools to the 60s. Unfortunately, the drop in temperature brings out mosquitoes that sometimes are difficult to distinguish from seagulls. In the evening, sorties of moths and formations of deerflies are chased by battalions of bats, ensuring that an open deck remains relatively unusable.

Then there's winter in Maine. It gets cold here. Very cold. To help with heating costs, you need all of the south-facing windows you can get. So shading those windows with a permanent roof over a screened-in porch that's only useful three months out of the year is counterproductive. Besides, such a roof would create a gloomy, sunless living room, which in my house is the south-facing room adjacent to the deck. So the idea of a seasonal screened-in porch was born.

Choose the Right Type of Beams

I couldn't find a design for such a porch in any architecture book, so I fell back on my own building knowledge, particularly my post-and-beam background and some of my boatbuilding experience.

The post-and-beam approach seemed the best way to achieve the required basic strength without a lot of studs to clutter the view. A minimum of framing members also would simplify assembly and disassembly. Because the load on these posts and beams would be no more than the weight of the galvanized steel-tubing awning frame and the awning itself, 4x4 top plates and posts would be more than sufficient.

Still, I had to keep everything lightweight for easy assembly and disassembly by one person. I also knew that posts would absorb rainwater along their bottom edges like sponges. So the post-and-beam structure would also have to be highly rot-resistant. These requirements forced me to rule out

Simple Connections Make This Porch Easy to Put Up and Knock Down

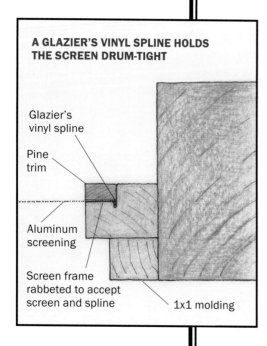

A GLAZIER'S VINYL SPLINE HOLDS THE SCREEN DRUM-TIGHT

Glazier's vinyl spline

Pine trim

Aluminum screening

Screen frame rabbeted to accept screen and spline

1x1 molding

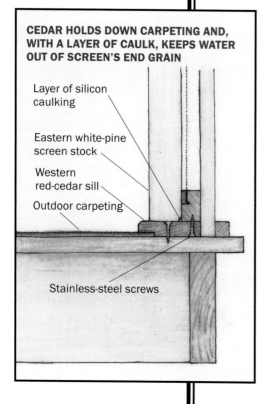

CEDAR HOLDS DOWN CARPETING AND, WITH A LAYER OF CAULK, KEEPS WATER OUT OF SCREEN'S END GRAIN

Layer of silicon caulking

Eastern white-pine screen stock

Western red-cedar sill

Outdoor carpeting

Stainless-steel screws

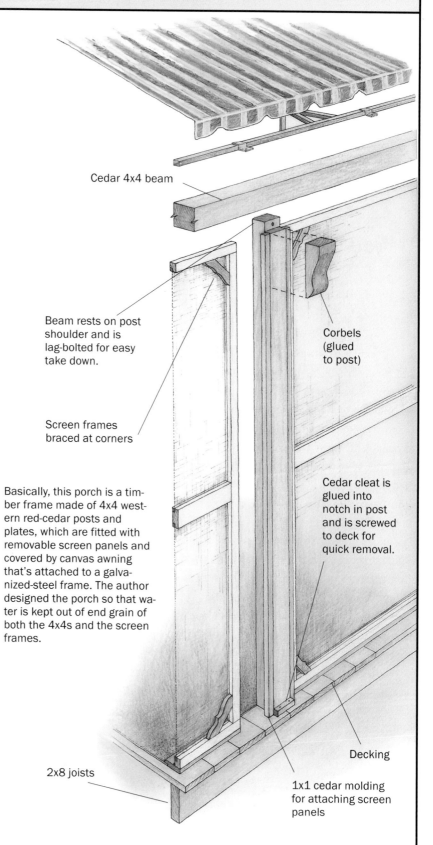

Cedar 4x4 beam

Beam rests on post shoulder and is lag-bolted for easy take down.

Screen frames braced at corners

Corbels (glued to post)

Cedar cleat is glued into notch in post and is screwed to deck for quick removal.

Basically, this porch is a timber frame made of 4x4 western red-cedar posts and plates, which are fitted with removable screen panels and covered by canvas awning that's attached to a galvanized-steel frame. The author designed the porch so that water is kept out of end grain of both the 4x4s and the screen frames.

Decking

2x8 joists

1x1 cedar molding for attaching screen panels

pressure-treated pine. Although available and inexpensive, it's too heavy and prone to movement during the humidity swings common during summers on the Maine coast.

The need for a light, durable wood led me to cedar. I could've used local northern white cedar, but I settled on western red cedar as the best solution. It's more straight-grained than local cedar, and clear 4x4s are readily available in lengths up to 20 ft. California redwood also was a possibility, but it's slightly more expensive than western red cedar and would have taken longer to get delivered.

Diverting Water away from the Existing Deck

The deck I planned to screen in was 12 ft. by 16 ft. The decking was eastern spruce, which made it a good surface for solidly attaching a temporary structure. Spruce holds screws well, an important attribute for the design I had in mind, but it's not very rot-resistant, a point that forced me to adjust the design to keep water from being trapped between the screens and posts and the decking.

To do this, I offset the top plate by 2½ in., creating a small overhang on 4x4 posts, enough to keep the daily summer trickles of dew and drizzly fog from coursing down the screens and posts. Although the posts were securely notched and bolted to the top plate, I added a corbel to help support the top plate and soften the generally boxy look of the frame.

At the bottom of the posts, I needed a lip through which I could securely fasten the post to the deck. Rather than use some sort of angle iron or metal bracket, I notched out a space at the bottom of the post. Then I glued and screwed a piece of western red cedar in the notch. In addition to eliminating the potentially ugly angle bracket, the cedar lip also cut down on the amount of water-absorbing end grain surface at the post bottom.

For additional rigidity, I used diagonal beams at the outside corners of the top plates (photo, above). I also used a bracing beam down the middle of the structure to stabilize the outer wall top plate and to make one more surface on which the awning frame would rest.

Avoid Iron Hardware

As a former boatbuilder, I decided that all of the bolts, screws and hardware in this project should be nonferrous. From long experience, I knew that even galvanized-iron hardware breaks down and starts to stain badly after a few years of coastal weather. The local hardware store carried a variety of stainless-steel hardware. But if you live away from the coast, a marine catalog can supply what you need.

Boatbuilding experience also led me to choose a two-part resorcinol glue for all of the joints on the screens and for attaching the corbels to the tops of the posts. Epoxy is a fine waterproof glue. But with most epoxies, you run the risk of joints becoming glue-

starved. This condition happens when the two pieces of wood being joined are mated so well that too much of the epoxy is squeezed out under modest clamping pressure, weakening the joint. Resorcinol, however, works best in tight joints.

Screen-Making Isn't Simple

Construction of the screens seemed like a pretty straightforward process of making frames and putting screens into them. Fortunately, I talked with a local glazier first and learned a little about screens before I made some common mistakes.

The size of the screen area is important. To end up with drum-tight screens, it's important to keep the openings as small as possible. The absolutely largest opening in a screened wall or door should be no bigger than 3½ ft. by 5 ft. Larger than that, it's hard to keep the screen surface from bulging the first time it's bumped.

CHOOSE GOOD STOCK

Screen stock also needs to be strong, light and durable. So I chose eastern white pine, the traditional stock for screen lumber. Western red cedar seems too brittle, even if I could have found the 5/4 and 6/4 rough stock. (As a general rule, the minimum finished thickness for screen stock should be 1 in. for screened walls, and 1¼ in. for screened doors.)

In constructing the screened walls, I used 1½-in.-wide stock around the edges, knowing the screen would gain additional rigidity when screwed into the top beam, posts and deck (photo, left). Likewise, the decorative diagonals at the corners of the screened frames would lend rigidity to the post-and-beam structure. I increased the size of the rail, dividing the upper and lower screen to 3 in. to compensate for its general lack of support.

Wide screen stock and corner brackets prevent bulging screens, which are further stiffened when the screens are screwed into place. The cedar sill at the bottom of the screen holds down the carpeting and keeps water from the frame.

All of the screened-frame and screened-door joints were half laps, which increased the structure's overall strength. Although mortise and tenon is the traditional joint and although modern methods tempted me to use biscuit joints at the corners, the additional strength of the half laps seemed worth the extra effort.

ADD A SPLINE TO THE RABBET

The rabbet for the screening itself seemed simple enough until the glaziers at Coastal Glass in Bath, Maine, straightened me out. I was simply going to rout a rabbet ⅜ in. wide and ⁵⁄₁₆ in. deep. But to make the screening tight in the opening, glaziers now use a vinyl spline inside the rabbet (top left drawing, p. 46). With the spline in place and the rabbet trim nailed home, the screen has little give at the edges and tends to remain tight.

To make the additional rabbet for the glazier's vinyl spline, I used a circular saw with a carbon-tipped finish blade in it, set it to the proper depth, set the blade guard against the screen frame and cut the spline groove.

INCLUDE A CEDAR LIP

The final step in constructing the screened frames was the addition of a cedar securing lip at the bottom of each frame. This step served three purposes: It gave me a lip, or sill, to use to screw the screen to the deck; it provided a means to hold down the outdoor carpeting; and it kept the screen edge a little farther away from water that might pool during rainstorms. I screwed the cedar lip to the bottom edge of the screen after I set the edge in silicone caulk to keep the pine frame from absorbing water (bottom left drawing, p. 46).

I ripped 1-in. by 1-in. strips of cedar and mounted them along the inside top and sides of the posts. The screen panels are then screwed into these strips. One final note on screens: I advise against installing the screening yourself. Even professional glaziers have trouble keeping screening tight while they are setting the vinyl spline and stapling everything home. It's definitely a two-man job even for the pros, particularly with large screened surfaces. We chose charcoal-finish aluminum screening over shiny aluminum, nylon, or brass.

Of Bugs, Rugs, and Awnings

If you build a seasonal screened porch, it's wise to work closely with the company that will make and install the awning and its frame. Blackfoot Awning & Canvas in nearby Auburn, Maine, made several trips to the job site to double-check measurements and to discuss exactly how I wanted the awning to fit.

Many custom-awning companies work largely on storefront overhangs. Galvanized-steel frames support these awnings, which are usually laced down. For a screened-in porch, however, loose lacings would allow bugs to sneak inside. Instead, Blackfoot Awning used strips of Velcro® where the awning met the wooden top plate. This construction effectively kept out the bugs.

Keeping bugs out also meant that we had to buy indoor-outdoor carpeting to cover the deck. When you buy the carpeting, be sure to ask about shrinkage. Hot sun will make some synthetic carpeting shrink. If so, buy a piece a little bigger than you need and cut it to size only after it's been in the sun a few days.

Finally, be careful to specify that the awning frame be lightweight and easily managed by one person. The welded frame for my porch could have been divided into three sections instead of two, making it easier for me to handle during breakdown and setup. In two sections, each piece is probably no more than 50 lb. But because of their bulk, they're awkward for one person to handle. If you add extra frame sections, use additional beams to support the additional sections.

With the vinyl spline in place and the rabbet trim nailed home, the screen has little give at the edges and tends to remain tight.

TIP

When you buy the carpeting, be sure to ask about shrinkage. Hot sun will make some synthetic carpeting shrink. Buy a piece a little bigger than you need and cut it to size after it's been in the sun a few days.

Although the two sections of awning frame for the author's porch weigh only about 50 lb. apiece, they are unwieldy because of their size. One person can handle the frame, but it works better with two people on the job. If the frame had been in three sections instead of two, another beam would have been necessary.

Knockdown, Storage, and Costs

At the end of the summer season, I decided to knock down my screened porch, post-and-beam frame included. Although the frame could survive winter's worst weather, taking it down is so simple that there's really no point in leaving it up.

Knocking the structure down took about three hours. I had some help during the process. But I doubt doing it by myself would have taken much more than an extra half hour. Two people could have it all down and stored in two hours. Other than the awning frames, no piece weighed more than 15 lbs.

The cost of the project was $2,200, including the all-weather carpeting, the awning, and the frame. (The awning cost $1,000; the wood cost $550; the carpet cost $150; and miscellaneous glue and hardware cost $150.) The time to build all of the wooden parts worked out to about 14 working days for one person. The lion's share of that time was spent on the screens. There are, however, a few custom wooden screen manufacturers still around. That, of course, would probably double your costs.

*Price estimates noted are from 1996.

Ken Textor is an author and woodworker in Arrowsic, Maine.

Deck Design

■ BY SCOTT GROVE

A properly built deck should last a lifetime. But for this to be possible, you must constantly think about nature's elements as you design and build it. If you don't, trapped moisture can promote bacterial degrade that will slowly eat your deck away.

Planning the Deck

A deck is an intermediate space between the controlled environment of a house and the raw elements outdoors. Since a deck can expand the living area of the house and serve as an entry, it's important to consider traffic patterns in your planning. Avoid paths that cross through activity areas and arrange for them to be as direct as possible. A path improperly located can isolate small areas and render them nearly useless.

A deck can accentuate the good features of an area and minimize the bad ones. It can conceal a fuel tank or snuggle around a tree. Decks are great for hiding ugly foundations, service meters, or old concrete patios. Let these existing elements influence your deck design and they'll make your job easier.

Decks ease the transition between the house and the landscape and also serve as an entry. Properly designed so they won't trap water, they will withstand the destructive forces of the weather.

Planning the layout and orientation of a deck is at least as important as building it.

Safety is an important consideration when designing a deck. For instance, a landing in front of a door needs plenty of room to allow the door to open with at least one person on the landing. A low walkway that may be just fine without a railing in the summer can be dangerous in the winter, when snow conceals its edges. Define these edges and all corners, using posts, trees, bushes, rocks, or any other visual device on or off the deck that will help make the feature more obvious.

Designing a deck can seem complex if you've never built one before, so beginners should make a detailed drawing of the entire layout, board by board. Once the design is on paper, it's fairly easy to compile a list of materials. Planning the layout and orientation of a deck is at least as important as building it.

Estimating Costs

We've been building decks in New York State for seven years, and we use the following figures for rough estimates of the materials and labor needed to build a deck: $8 per sq. ft. for decking (including the framing and footings), $7 per sq. ft. for stairs, $10 per lin. ft. for simple railings, $15 per lin. ft. for bevel-cut railings, and $20 per lin. ft. for benches. These figures reflect our company's wage scale, construction speed, and craftsmanship. If a deck design is particularly unusual, we'll adjust the figures upward. For those who work alone or with minimal help, the following materials-only estimate, based on prices for #1 pressure-treated lumber in New York State, will help determine approximate costs: $3.00 per sq. ft. for the decking lumber, $4.50 per sq. ft. for stairs, $2.25 per lin. ft. for railings, and $8.25 per lin. ft. for benches. The type of construction you use, and the level of detail you include, will have a significant effect on the expense of your deck.

Choosing Lumber

Water is the worst enemy of woodwork, and this fact should be foremost in your mind as you select lumber for your deck. Remember that water does the most damage when it rests undisturbed on or in the wood, especially in places that are slow to dry out. Warping is the number one problem with decks, and water contributes to the problem. Checks channel water inside a board to accelerate the decay process, and so when we're building a deck we routinely cut back boards with serious end checks. We allow for these cuts when we design a deck by making sure that our plans call for material about 6 in. shorter than standard lumber lengths.

MOISTURE CONTENT

The amount of moisture within new lumber determines how much it will shrink. In wood that's continually exposed to the weather, shrinkage can be considerable. Try to buy kiln-dried lumber, even if this means purchasing from a supplier other than the one you usually use. If dry wood is not available, or if its added cost is not in your budget, at least make sure that the moisture content is consistent throughout your selection. You may not be able to prevent shrinkage, but if you plan for it ahead of time the deck will look better because the gaps between the boards will look uniform. Different-size gaps will make the work look sloppy.

GRADE AND SPECIES

The grade and species of lumber you select will directly affect the longevity of your deck. In parts of the west, decks are frequently built from cedar or redwood. These species are readily available and quite resistant to decay. But in the eastern part of the country, pressure-treated lumber is used most often because it withstands our harsh climate and is generally more available and less expensive than cedar or redwood.

There are two grades of pressure-treated lumber suitable for decks. We strongly recommend using #1 yellow pine, particularly for the railings, benches, and decking. The quality of #1 pressure-treated lumber is fairly consistent, and the material is easier to work than #2 grade. The #2 grade has a greater number of open knots and these weaken the boards and encourage water to accumulate. Large knots that span more than half the width of a board are very dangerous in either grade, since the pressure of a footstep or rough handling during construction will sometimes snap the board in half. One problem with pressure-treated lumber is warpage. It can twist severely, cup and bow if not handled correctly. Keep it covered and out of the sun until you use it.

Pressure-treated lumber often has a greenish color, due to the chemicals it's impregnated with (usually chromated copper arsenate). This tint will weather away into a pleasing light gray in about two years, though the treatment chemicals still protect the wood. Some people want more color to their deck, however, so we recommend a semitransparent stain. If you wait a year or so before the first application, the wood will have a chance to dry out and will accept a fuller coating, doubling the stain's expected life. We prefer stain to paint because paint traps moisture and requires more maintenance.

ORDERING

When you order the lumber for a deck, include about 10% more than you think you'll need. This will prevent time-consuming trips to the lumberyard if your estimate was slightly off and will allow you to cull out badly warped boards with too many knots.

When the lumber is delivered, remember that moist lawns and delivery trucks are a bad combination. There are better ways to find out where the septic-system drainfield is than to have a truck crush the drain tiles. And since the chemicals in pressure-treated lumber can kill grass, make sure you relocate lumber piles after three days to a different location on the lawn.

Nails

We use only galvanized nails on deck projects, 10d for the decking and 16d for framing. Two types of galvanized nails are available. Electroplated nails have a smooth finish and take less effort to pound in, but hot-dipped nails, with their rough surface, grip much better and are more rust-resistant. To save time in laying down decking, we use a pneumatic nailer and resin-coated galvanized nails. The resin coating heats up when the nail penetrates the wood, and then hardens like glue for a firm grip.

If you have problems with lumber splitting as you nail into it, use your hammer to blunt the end of your nails. This way they will puncture the wood instead of piercing and splitting it.

Piers

Like the foundation of a house, the foundation of a deck must transfer loads from the structure to the ground. But unlike the foundations of most houses, deck foundations are not continuous. To support the deck, a system of concrete piers is used. The piers extend from grade level to below the frost line—32 in. to 48 in. in our climate. A pier that does not go below the frost line will eventually heave and push the deck out of level.

LOCATING PIERS

The standard method of determining where the piers will go requires string, a collection of stakes, and the application of some basic practical geometry. This method works well on decks with simple rectilinear forms, but complex forms are considerably trickier to deal with. When we are faced with the task of building elaborate forms, we've found a way to locate piers that works quite well and that allows for design flexibility as the project progresses.

Rather than spend a lot of time and effort to locate all the piers at once, we use a locate-build-locate process. The idea is to

Remember that water does the most damage when it rests undisturbed on or in the wood, especially in places that are slow to dry out.

TIP

To save time in laying down decking, use a pneumatic nailer and resin-coated galvanized nails. The resin coating heats up when the nail penetrates the wood, and then hardens like glue for a firm grip.

define the limits of the deck, locate and then pour perimeter piers. Once this is done we can frame the perimeter of the deck, bracing it in place. After that, we locate the rest of the piers.

The easiest piers to locate are the ones that must be placed at a particular point. If you know, for example, that you want the edge of the deck to change direction about 10 ft. from the house and 14 ft. from the oak tree, dig and pour a pier there. The process is empirical: You build what you know to answer questions about what you don't know.

After the concrete has partially cured in about 24 hours (it will take nearly a month to gain most of its strength), we begin framing. This method may seem somewhat backward, but we often find it much easier and more accurate in the long run to dig some piers to support interior spans after the perimeter is established.

TOOLS FOR DIGGING PIERS

You will need a long-handled shovel, a digging bar, and a post-hole digger to dig the holes for the piers. There are two kinds of manually operated post-hole diggers, and you may end up using both of them on your deck project. A post-hole auger looks and works somewhat like a giant corkscrew; as you turn it into the earth, it pulls dirt from the hole. An auger works particularly well in hard ground but is easily stymied by rocks. A clamshell post-hole digger looks like two long-handled spades hinged together at the ferrule, with the blades opposing each other. The work goes quickly in soft ground, but more slowly in packed or clay soils. The clamshell is less likely to stall when you hit rocks, because it can reach into a hole to remove them, but large rocks can cause problems.

If you have a lot of holes to dig, you can rent a gasoline-powered hole digger. This is basically a power auger, and we prefer the one-person model with a torque bar because it won't take you for a ride when it hits a rock.

A long digging bar comes in handy for loosening dirt and breaking rocks that can't easily be removed from the hole in one piece. It also helps loosen tightly packed soil. This solid, heavy steel persuader is pointed on one end and can also be used to pry out rocks.

Rocks are the main problem in digging footings around here, but roots can also be a nuisance, since decks are frequently near large trees. Use an old handsaw or sharp ax to cut the roots cleanly, but don't seal the cut ends. A botanist once told me that a root or branch will heal itself and that tar and other sealants interfere with this process.

The shape of the holes you dig is nearly as important as the depth. They should generally be round, and about 8 in. to 12 in. in diameter. The sides of the hole should be reasonably smooth, and the bottom of the hole should be slightly larger than the top to distribute loads well. If there are any ledges or if the hole narrows at the bottom, the freeze/thaw cycle will lift or tip the pier as much as 12 in. over time. Make sure that the bottom of the hole is undisturbed earth, because a layer of soft earth here will allow the pier to sink.

POURING CONCRETE

We usually pour concrete directly into the hole, using the sides of the hole to form the pier. You can also use Sonotubes® to line the hole. These cardboard tubes, available in various diameters from masonry-supply stores, are especially handy if you want the concrete to extend above grade to form a pier. If you suspend the tube 6 in. above the bottom of the hole when you pour, the concrete will ooze out the bottom to widen the base of the pier increasing its bearing ability. Piers should include #4 reinforcing bar if they extend more than 6 in. above grade.

A good concrete mix for piers is 1:2:3, which means one part portland cement, two parts sand, and three parts gravel (¾-in. or 1-in. gravel will be fine). An alternative to mixing your own concrete is to purchase ready-mix, which is a preproportioned

> *A good concrete mix for piers is 1:2:3, which means one part portland cement, two parts sand, and three parts gravel.*

cement, gravel, and sand mixture that usually comes in 90-lb. bags. The portland cement will sometimes settle to the bottom of ready-mix bags, so it's a good idea to dry-mix the contents of each bag before adding water. A wheelbarrow is great for mixing concrete in, but be sure to wash it out afterwards, along with your mixing tools.

The Ledger

The ledger is a length of 2x lumber that is attached directly to the house, allowing a portion of the deck to "borrow" the foundation of the house for support. It's usually the first framing member to be installed and should be selected from the straightest stock available, since it serves as a reference point for much of the work to follow. When you install the ledger, don't rely on the house siding or the foundation to be level, because often they're not.

The top of the ledger supports the decking, and if you think of it as a rim joist, you'll get the idea. If the ledger has to be attached to the house foundation in order for the final deck elevation to be where you want it, you'll have to fasten it with lag bolts and lead expansion shields or some other masonry-anchor system. Masonry nails won't work very well, particularly in poured foundations that have had many years to cure. When using a standard masonry bit in an electric drill to bore holes for the expansion shields in a concrete foundation, use a star drill to break apart any pieces of aggregate you can't drill through. We've found that a roto-hammer speeds this job considerably.

Sometimes the plans will call for the ledger to be fastened above the house foundation, and in this case, 4-in. by ⅜-in. galvanized lag bolts spaced about 24 in. apart and fastened to studs or a rim joist will usually do the job. Slide flashing under the existing siding and over the ledger, if possible, to keep water from seeping behind it. If the ledger is going to be mounted to some sort of concrete patio or walkway, use shims to

Finding Level

Building a deck can be an exercise in elementary civil engineering, and many beginners are frustrated by having to find the proper relationship between posts and boards that aren't connected. You can't always use a carpenter's level to do this—how would you check two posts, 15 ft. apart, to see if they are at the same height? We often use a 2-ft. level on a long, straight board to check for level, but other tools can be used as well.

A string level is a small spirit level that hooks onto a length of layout twine. When the twine is pulled taut, a rough estimate of level can be determined by raising or lowering one end of the twine and watching the bubble in the level.

An optical pocket level is something of a cross between a telescope and a transit. Looking through it, you align a small leveling bubble with cross hairs to determine an approximately level visual line.

A water level is an inexpensive and very accurate homemade device used to check the relative heights of widely separated items. It's made from clear plastic tubing filled with water (a few drops of food color will make the water easier to see). Because of atmospheric pressure, the water level at one end of the tubing always matches the water level at the opposite end, no matter how many twists and turns the tubing takes. It's particularly useful over long distances, as when you want to compare the heights of ledger and posts.

A transit is a precision instrument used by surveyors, and this is what we use to determine level, plumb, and the relative heights of widely distant objects with a high degree of accuracy. A transit is fairly expensive, but if you do a lot of decks, the money is well spent.

DECKING
Use 2x4s, 2x6s, or alternate each. Laying boards at an angle increases the rigidity of the deck. Line up the joints, and place them over the gap in doubled joists. To eliminate water collection on top, leave a ⅛-in. to ¼-in. gap between boards. Nail twice at each joist with 10d galvanized casing nails.

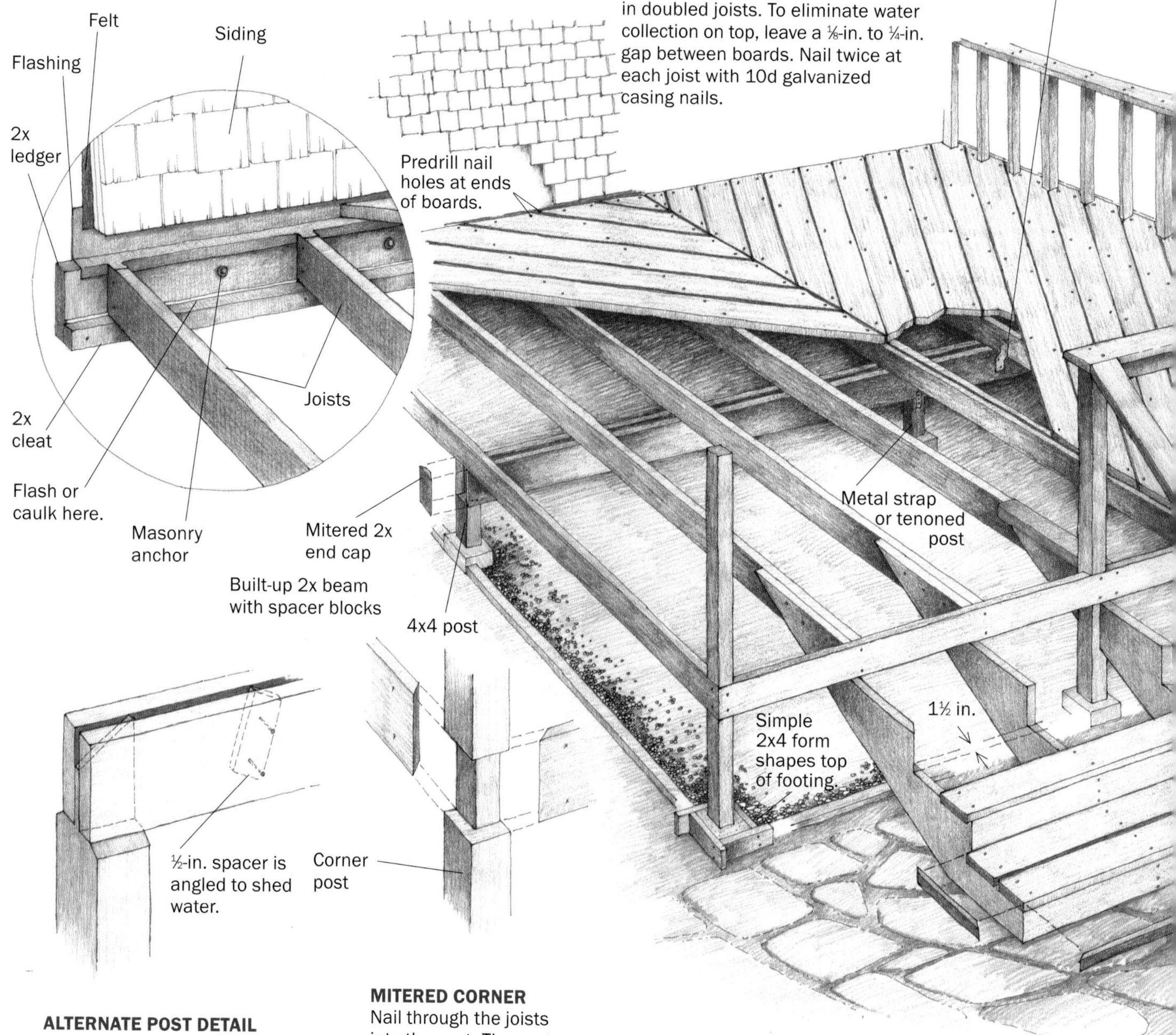

Anchor joists with metal ties, or toenail.

Felt

Flashing

Siding

2x ledger

Predrill nail holes at ends of boards.

Joists

2x cleat

Flash or caulk here.

Masonry anchor

Mitered 2x end cap

Metal strap or tenoned post

Built-up 2x beam with spacer blocks

4x4 post

1½ in.

Simple 2x4 form shapes top of footing.

½-in. spacer is angled to shed water.

Corner post

ALTERNATE POST DETAIL
A 6x6 post is notched to support doubled 2x joists or a built-up beam. The tongue and the shoulders of the post should be beveled to shed water.

MITERED CORNER
Nail through the joists into the post. The post can be extended to provide railing support.

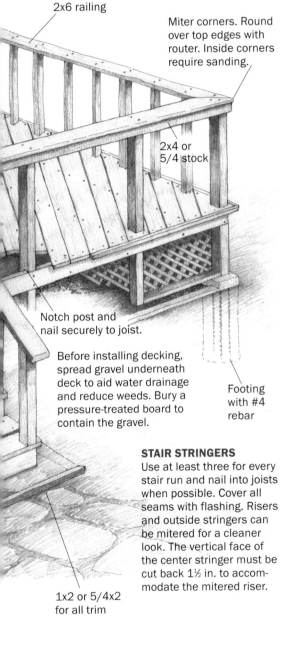

Use 16d nails for structural nailing and 10d for decking and toenailing.

2x6 railing

Miter corners. Round over top edges with router. Inside corners require sanding.

2x4 or 5/4 stock

Notch post and nail securely to joist.

Before installing decking, spread gravel underneath deck to aid water drainage and reduce weeds. Bury a pressure-treated board to contain the gravel.

Footing with #4 rebar

STAIR STRINGERS
Use at least three for every stair run and nail into joists when possible. Cover all seams with flashing. Risers and outside stringers can be mitered for a cleaner look. The vertical face of the center stringer must be cut back 1½ in. to accommodate the mitered riser.

1x2 or 5/4x2 for all trim

hold the board away from the concrete to allow the water to pass freely by.

Allow at least 1 in. between door sills and the decking surface to prevent any water from running back off the deck into the house. If you include a step, use the same step rise used elsewhere on the deck for the sake of consistency.

Posts

Posts transfer the loads from the deck structure to the piers. One end of each post is attached to a beam or a joist, and the other end rests on the pier. We usually don't anchor posts to the piers, since the weight of the deck is enough to keep them in position. Though many people embed posts in concrete, we feel this technique can create serious problems if water collects between the post and the concrete. Posts are usually 4x4s, 4x6s or 6x6s. A 6x6 post is generally more than needed for bearing purposes, but it enables us to notch beams or joists into it for added strength.

Beams

Beams are an intermediate structural member, used to support joists. They can be solid lumber, usually 4x6 or 4x8, or they can be built up out of 2x lumber. When you're fabricating built-up beams, a common mistake is to nail the individual 2x material face to face, which allows water to get trapped between these boards. Instead, you should sandwich blocks of ½-in. pressure-treated wood between the boards to create a void for water to run through.

Joists

Joists are the uppermost structural element supporting the decking. They are generally 2x lumber and should be reasonably straight. When laying joists into place, make sure that any crown in the board is facing up; in time, gravity and the weight of the decking will straighten the joists.

When laying joists into place, make sure that any crown in the board is facing up; in time, gravity and the weight of the decking will straighten the joists.

The premature failure of decking is often caused by nailing too close to the end of the board. This encourages splitting and allows water to accumulate around the board ends.

There are at least two good techniques for attaching joists to the ledger and at least one that should not be used. One reason many decks decay at this location is that the joists are toenailed into the ledger; nails split the ends of the joists, allowing water to collect exactly where it shouldn't. Joist hangers minimize splitting at the joist end and will prevent water from getting trapped in this crucial joint. We first nail the hangers to the joists and then fit the assembly to a level chalkline. This compensates for slight variations in joist width.

A cleat can also be used to support the ends of the joists. You still need to toenail the joists, but splitting is reduced because the nails can be a smaller size since they do not carry the weight of the deck. If you use this technique, the ledger should be one dimension wider than the joists. For example, use a 2x8 ledger with 2x6 joists. This will allow room for a 2x2 cleat to be attached to the ledger. Run a bead of silicone caulk along the cleat/ledger seam to keep the water out.

Decking

If the decking surface is not applied properly, it will be the first thing to deteriorate, causing a chain reaction of decay throughout the rest of the structure. *Never* butt the ends of two decking members together and nail into a single joist. This is one of the major causes of decking failure. The reason is that water collects in the seam between the butting boards and enters their end grain. And when two boards butt over a single joist, the problem is intensified. With only ¾ in. for each deck board to be nailed into, the nails must be placed very close to the end of the board, encouraging splitting.

We get around these problems by doubling up strategic joists, using a block of wood between them to create a 1½-in. space. The end of each deck board cantilevers over this space so water can't collect. This also allows the boards to be nailed farther from their ends, which minimizes splitting. If you must nail closer than 2 in. to the end of a board, predrilling the nail holes can also help reduce splitting.

For the decking surface, we like to use 2x6s or sometimes 5/4x6s if the quality is good. You can also use 2x4s, but you'll have a lot more nailing to do. If you have the choice, nail the decking cup-side down to prevent any water from pooling on the individual boards.

We like to space the decking boards about ⅛ in. apart (the thickness of a 10d nail). The boards will shrink, depending on their moisture content, and we have seen this space expand up to ¼ in. If there are a lot of deciduous trees with small leaves close to the deck, you might want a wider spacing to allow the leaves to fall through. When you're installing the decking, some boards will most likely be crooked. With a flat bar and some lever action, one person can easily straighten out each board while nailing.

Stairways

Stairways can be dangerous areas and require special attention. Codes usually call for at least one railing at the side of the stairs if they include more than two risers. Wide stairways have a spacious and inviting appearance, so we like to build them at least 4 ft. wide, enough for two people to pass comfortably.

Inconsistency in the height of a step or length of a tread is dangerous and awkward. We have found that a shorter rise and longer tread is easier to walk up, safer, and more elegant. A rise of about 7 in. seems to make a comfortable step and allows us to use an untrimmed 2x6 for the risers. Sometimes we miter the riser boards into the outside stringers. We're not fond of exposed stringers. We use a pair of 2x6s for the tread; these make a run of a bit more than 12 in. with a trim board.

We use three stringers for deck stairs, even if the stairway is only 30 in. wide. We have seen too many stairways warp and fall apart with only two stringers. Using three-stringer construction isn't too difficult and doesn't cost much more. In fact, the trickiest part of building one is cutting each stringer to identical shape and lining them all up in the same plane on the rise and run.

You can buy framing clips (called stair gauge buttons) to keep your framing square in the right position while you lay out each stringer, but this doesn't always get you past Murphy's law. Our trick is to lay out one stringer only and clamp it to another length of stringer stock. When you cut the first one, the sawblade scores the second one, saving you one layout. Repeat the process with additional stringers. This will duplicate all the stringers and save layout time.

Railings

Railings are important to the safety and appearance of decks. As a design element, they can be the highlight and outline of your project. Railings are one of the places where

Cutting the decking to length after nailing it in place ensures a clean, uniform edge and saves time otherwise spent cutting boards one by one. Run the boards long and snap a chalkline to mark the cutting path, or use a straightedge to guide the shoe of the saw.

a designer's creativity can be expressed, and there is no one way to build them. But there are some general rules to follow.

The most important characteristic of a good railing is strength. You can be sure that people will lean against the railing, and often they will sit on it, too. A strong railing is particularly important on elevated decks. We like to play it safe and build our railings as strong as possible. To do this, we solidly attach the posts or balusters to the deck joists. These structural supports should be located no more than 48 in. apart, and the railing should be about 34 in. above the decking surface. Be sure that the edges of the railing are well sanded, especially in places that will get a lot of use, such as stair railings.

TIP

If there are a lot of deciduous trees with small leaves close to the deck, you might want to space the decking boards more than ⅛ in. apart to allow the leaves to fall through.

Bench supports built from 2x8s can be trimmed to a width of about 3½ in. where they form the backrest. The supports should be securely nailed or bolted to the deck's supporting structure.

Consider the spacing between your railing uprights as part of the project's visual design. Close spacing visually encloses the space and prevents small children from falling through. Railings with fewer uprights will visually expand the space and be less inhibiting to your view.

One type of railing we use combines a bevel-cut 2x6 and a matching 2x4 into an L shape. We position the 2x6 horizontally, and our clients enjoy the strong visual effect this creates. The 2x6 acts as a cap for the railing uprights, shielding their end grain from the elements. Although tricky, this technique allows for some very interesting joinery at all corners. To clean up the mitered edge, we round it over with a router or belt sander.

Seating

Built-in seating is a great way to finish the deck. As with railings, there are many ways to build it, and no one way is correct.

You can build seating either with or without a backrest, and the choice will often depend on whether or not an unobstructed view is important. If comfort is more important, you'll want to build at least some of the seats with a backrest. The top of the backrest should be between 30 in. and 34 in. from the deck, which can be designed nicely to tie in with the railing.

A backless bench can function as a physical barrier for a deck edge without acting as a visual barrier as well. We have also used a low, wide railing as a mini-bench, which also makes a good place to display potted plants. And sometimes we'll use a built-in planter to serve as a visual barrier.

Benches can be difficult to build, since they not only have to be strong but comfortable too. With backless benches, we have used 4x4s or 2x6s as supports. For a bench with a backrest, we use a 2x8 as the seat support and rip it down to a 2x4 for the backrest support. A 15° backward lean seems to be comfortable. We then run our mitered railing across the top at 32 in. The cross supports for the seat are 2x6s cut into long, wide triangles. For the seat, we use three 2x6s with a 2x4 band. This will give the seat a total width of 18 in. The standard seat height that we use is 17 in. In calculating seating height, don't forget to account for any cushions that you might use. Save your best boards for construction of the seating, because this part of the deck will be well used and very visible.

A Final Note

Use these tips in combination with your local codes. With a little creativity and your basic construction knowledge, the deck you build should last a long time.

*Price estimates noted are from 1985.

Scott Grove is a partner in Effective Design, a design/build company in Rochester, New York.

Choosing Materials for Exterior Decks

■ BY SCOTT GIBSON

Few alterations to a house are as welcome as a new exterior deck. Structurally sound, cosmetically pristine, a new deck invites dawdling, outdoor grilling, conversation, rustic contemplation, an extra hour with the Sunday paper. Blessed with such a structure, you have to remember only one thing. Before the last deck board goes down,

nature is already hard at work trying to destroy what you have wrought.

With no protection from rain or sunlight, exposure to wood-devouring insects and cycles of heat and cold, the deck is in an environment that is just plain unforgiving. It hardly matters whether the deck is a simple ground-level platform or a grand multilevel

Here's a sampling of the decking materials available today. From left to right: treated southern pine, redwood, Brock Deck® vinyl decking, treated fir, Trex® plastic composite decking, Nexwood plastic composite, ipé, and Dream Deck vinyl decking.

structure. They all sit out in the same weather. Unless rebuilding a deck every few years appeals to you, the design process ought to include finding decking that forestalls the aging process as long as possible while offering the best balance between cost and aesthetics.

Traditionally, decking has been wood. Depending on what part of the country you live in, that might be redwood, western red cedar or pressure-treated southern pine.

Other types of wood decking also are becoming easier to find: Alaska yellow cedar, rain-forest hardwoods such as ipé, and red meranti from Malaysia. In addition, two new categories of decking have appeared in recent years: composites of natural fiber and recycled plastic, and decking made entirely of extruded vinyl.

Treated Southern Pine Is Inexpensive but Prone to Movement

Treated southern pine's pale green hue, which fades to gray over time, comes from the chromated copper arsenate (CCA) that gives the wood its longevity. Treated pine could be any one of four species: longleaf, shortleaf, slash, or loblolly. For decking use, it is typically sold as 5/4x6-in. RED (radius-edge decking) in standard grade and premium grade.

Pressure-treated southern pine is one of the least expensive decking options around—about $1.25 per lin. ft. for 5/4x6-in. premium-grade RED, slightly less for standard.

CCA is the most common of several waterborne preservatives the USDA Forest Products Laboratory characterizes as "broad-spectrum pesticides." It renders wood unusable as a food source for insects and fungi. A retention level of 0.25 lb. of preservative per cu. ft. is suggested for lumber used above ground; lumber that will come into contact with the ground should be rated at 0.40 lb. per cu. ft.

Treated pine is relatively hard, but it has the reputation of moving around after it has been installed. Starting with dry lumber and applying a water repellent periodically will be a big help in reducing splitting, checking, and cupping. Your best bet is to look for decking that has been kiln dried or air dried after treatment, or air-dry it yourself before installing it.

In addition to CCA, a waxlike water repellent also is applied to some brands of treated pine.

Treated southern pine

Usually available on premium decking, it comes at a slightly higher cost. This treatment of repellent will save you the trouble of an initial application of water repellent, but it won't get you off the hook for good. A yearly reapplication of a good-quality water repellent is still recommended.

Because southern pine species accept a chemical treatment so readily, it is not necessary to field treat any end cuts or any holes that are made as the deck boards are installed.

Health warnings continue to dog CCA-treated wood, but risks seem relatively slight. The Southern Forest Products Association℠, a trade group, suggests commonsense precautions: Wash your hands after handling the material, wear a dust mask and eye protection when cutting it, and do not burn treated wood. While raw chemicals used in the treating process are "kind of rough," the association says, they bond well to wood and do not leach out easily. As one association official says, CCA treatment "is about the safest one we've got." For more consumer information on CCA, try the American Wood Preservers Institute's Web site.

water-repellent finish.) However, you can control the amount of moisture in the wood. Too much—or even too little—moisture in wood can eventually lead to structural problems.

Moisture Content Can Affect a Deck for Years

To minimize warping, splitting, checking, shrinking, and failing finish, the deck boards at the time of construction should be uniform and less than about 20% MC, regardless of the species or whether the wood has been pressure-treated.

In most areas of the United States, we expect lumber in aboveground, protected, exterior applications to reach an equilibrium moisture content (EMC) around 12%. If your specific site is normally either very wet or very dry, the EMC will be higher or lower, respectively.

In general, the moisture content of most treated lumber is high—in the 35% to 75% MC range—and the wood is still wet when it arrives at the job site, unless it has been kiln dried after treatment and marked KDAT. If the wood is stamped KDAT, its moisture content should be about 19% or less. Because redwood and cedar aren't treated with preservatives, they're usually marketed as kiln dried or as air seasoned, which means they will have about a 20% MC. Most deck builders install deck boards on delivery. Although this way is easiest, pressure-treated boards probably will vary greatly in moisture content and often will shrink unevenly.

In the case of preservative-treated wood, we recommend KDAT lumber, when available, because many problems that eventually surface in deck construction are a result of using wet lumber. Another option is to air-dry the treated lumber yourself. In both cases, you'll be able to identify problem deck boards before installation and exclude them from your project.

Air-dry Lumber to Equalize Moisture Content

Treated lumber that's not marked KDAT should be air-dried for several weeks, depending on the type of weather and the extent to which the lumber is exposed.

Usually, pressure-treated wood comes directly from the treater and is bound and shipped wet to the lumberyard, where it often is stored outside and unprotected. Air-drying for several weeks will help even out the moisture-content differences between the pieces of wood and, on average, will lead to a more consistent moisture content at installation.

In the long run, it is worthwhile to order the lumber to arrive at the job site a few weeks early to allow time for air-drying. Air-drying also is recommended if you build a deck with redwood or cedar that contains a moisture content much greater than 20%.

Many problems that eventually surface in deck construction are a result of using wet lumber.

TIP

Place weights, such as concrete blocks, on top of the pile of boards to help minimize twisting of lumber during drying, but avoid iron weights because they can stain the wood if they get wet.

To dry lumber properly, align the stickers, or spacer strips of wood, over pile supports to promote even weight distribution and optimal drying. Place weights on top of the stack of wood to stop the top boards from warping.

The air-drying method we recommend is stacking the lumber in layers separated by narrow strips of wood, or stickers, to allow air to move freely between layers. Care should be taken to align the stickers vertically within the pile. Alignment helps distribute the load evenly and minimize warping during drying. Also, it's a good idea to place weights, such as concrete blocks, on top of the pile to help minimize twisting of lumber during drying. (Avoid iron weights because they can stain the wood if they get wet.)

If the pile can be protected from the weather—either by a shed or by plastic sheeting—and is allowed to dry several weeks, the lumber should reach a moisture content of close to 20%.

Using an electronic moisture meter is a simple method of measuring moisture content in wood. This kind of meter typically measures the electrical resistance between two metal pins driven into the wood. Moisture meters must be calibrated, depending on wood species and temperature. You can purchase a moisture meter for around $100.

Moisture content also can be determined by weighing a few representative small pieces of wood, drying the pieces in an oven at 200°F for 24 hours and weighing them again after they're oven dry. Divide the difference between the original weight and the oven-dry weight by the oven-dry weight, then multiply by 100 to get the moisture content in the form of a percentage.

Shrinking Can Be Used to Your Benefit

Wood shrinks only when moisture content falls below about 30%. A 6-in.-wide treated southern pine deck board should shrink by about ³⁄₁₆ in. if it reaches 12% EMC, so laying wet decking boards tightly against each other should result in a ³⁄₁₆-in. gap when the boards dry. For redwood or cedar purchased at 20% MC, a nominal 6-in. decking board will shrink only about ¹⁄₁₀ in. when a 12% EMC is reached. If the lumber installed is drier than the local EMC, and if the boards

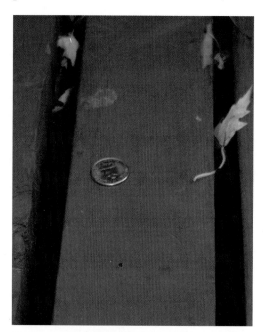

The gaps between these deck boards are much too great and can result in injury for women wearing high-heeled shoes or for small children. Gaps this wide can result when wet boards are laid with a gap between them. The gap becomes larger as the boards shrink.

Warping and cupping are usually caused by uneven shrinkage between the top surface and the bottom surface of wood. The wrong types or placement of fasteners also can cause wood to warp and cup, as shown above.

are laid tight, there's potential for the wood to pick up moisture, swell, and buckle.

Depending on the lumber species and moisture content—as well as the desired gap between boards—a gap between deck boards can be planned based on the amount of expected shrinkage. We suggest a final gap of about ¾₆ in. to ¼ in.—not big enough to catch a small heel, but big enough to allow dirt, leaves, and other debris to fall through.

Warping and cupping usually are caused by uneven shrinkage between the top surface and the bottom surface of deck lumber. The cupping of individual boards is aggravated because the top surface is usually at a lower moisture content—because of exposure to the sun and wind—compared with the protected bottom surface. This situation means that deck boards installed wet are likely to warp the most, especially when installed during hot months. This shrinkage difference is more pronounced if the bottoms of the boards remain damp, such as when the deck is built low to the ground or near wet soil.

Finally, we don't recommend using deck boards wider than 6 in. because cupping and warping can become excessive.

Don't Forget to Finish the Job

Even though you're using naturally decay-resistant or pressure-treated wood, the horizontal surface of a deck is exposed to foot traffic, sun, and rain, which makes finishing a deck with a water-repellent preservative a necessity. This exposure will degrade the wood's surface, and unless the wood receives the proper finish, discoloration and checking often result, leading to a rough, uneven deck surface and decay in untreated wood. Applying and maintaining a finish on your deck will help minimize problems.

It used to be recommended to wait a year, or a season, to finish a deck. In our experience, this amount of time is too long because surface problems that cannot be corrected later may develop (i.e., checking, cracking, splintering).

For a new deck, apply the finish after the surface of the wood has dried to about 20% MC. Wood stamped S-DRY, KD (kiln dried), MC-15 (average moisture content 15%), or KDAT has been dried and can be finished immediately.

Bob Falk, P.E., is a structural engineer and **Kent McDonald** and **Jerry Winandy** are wood scientists at the USDA Forest Products Laboratory in Madison, Wisconsin. They are co-authors of Wood Decks: Materials, Construction, and Finishing, *a handbook published in cooperation with the Forest Products Society (2801 Marshall Court, Madison, WI 53705; 608-231-1361 or www.forestprod.org).*

> Don't use deck boards wider than 6 in. because cupping and warping can become excessive.

Even cedar, redwood, and pressure-treated lumber require regular application of a water-repellent preservative (including mildewcide). Note the water intrusion around the long surface check of the leftmost deck board. In a year or two, this board will degrade to the same condition as the center board.

Details for a Lasting Deck

■ BY BOB FALK AND SAM WILLIAMS

Some decks need major overhauls after less than 10 years. Others stay strong and good looking for decades. What's the secret? Well, besides using suitable lumber (we recommend either a naturally durable species or preservative-treated lumber), a lasting deck is put together with strong, durable fasteners, and it gets regular applications of a penetrating finish to repel moisture and to minimize the effects of the weather.

Although the structure of a deck is a lot like the skeleton of a conventionally framed wood house, a deck doesn't have the stability of sheathing, and there's no roofing and siding to protect it from the elements. That's why decks require extra care and attention to detail. As wood researchers at the USDA Forest Products Laboratory, my colleagues and I have studied lumber, construction techniques, fasteners, and finishes. From this research, we offer some recommendations for building decks that last.

Start with Good Connections

In wood construction, connections often limit strength; so many common failures of deck construction lead back to connection performance. Proper connections of deck joists to beams, beams to posts, and decks to houses are critical.

Because fasteners and hardware in wood decks can corrode, it's prudent to minimize dependency on them. Wherever possible, joists and beams should bear directly on posts. This type of connection requires more vertical space, but it's more reliable than transferring load through fasteners.

There are a number of ways to connect beams to posts. Two-by lumber can be used as a beam if either set directly on top of the post or let into a notched post. This notched connection works only when the posts are 6x6 or better because notching a 4x4 post with 2x side members leaves only ½ in. of post for you to bolt through.

A better option when supporting a built-up beam with a 4x4 post is nailing a ½-in. treated-wood spacer between the two 2xs and setting the beam directly on the post. You also can tie the connection together with a hot-dipped galvanized beam-to-post connector. Just remember, though, that whenever you cut notches or install lag screws or bolts in deck lumber—even if it's preservative-treated lumber—you should treat the openings in the lumber with a wood preservative.

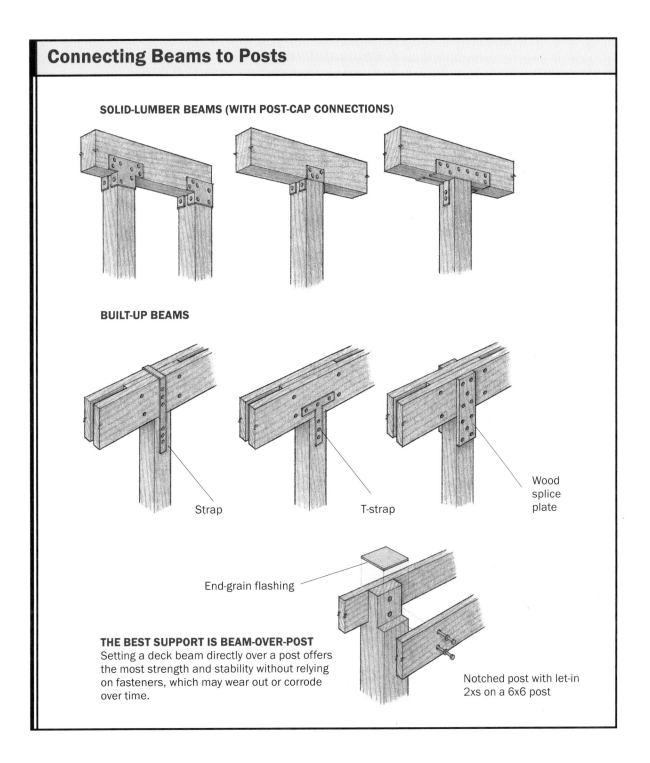

SOLID-LUMBER BEAMS (WITH POST-CAP CONNECTIONS)

BUILT-UP BEAMS

Strap

T-strap

Wood splice plate

End-grain flashing

THE BEST SUPPORT IS BEAM-OVER-POST
Setting a deck beam directly over a post offers the most strength and stability without relying on fasteners, which may wear out or corrode over time.

Notched post with let-in 2xs on a 6x6 post

The Connection at the House Must Be Detailed Carefully

Attaching a deck to a house is risky business. Screwing or bolting into a house opens the siding's protective envelope to moisture, which can lead to decay and insect attack.

Wherever practical, it's best to build a freestanding deck.

If a freestanding deck isn't feasible, take extra care attaching the deck to the house. And although it probably goes without saying, nails aren't adequate to make this connection.

To prevent water from entering the house, it's important to caulk pilot holes in the band

Space and Flash the Connection Properly

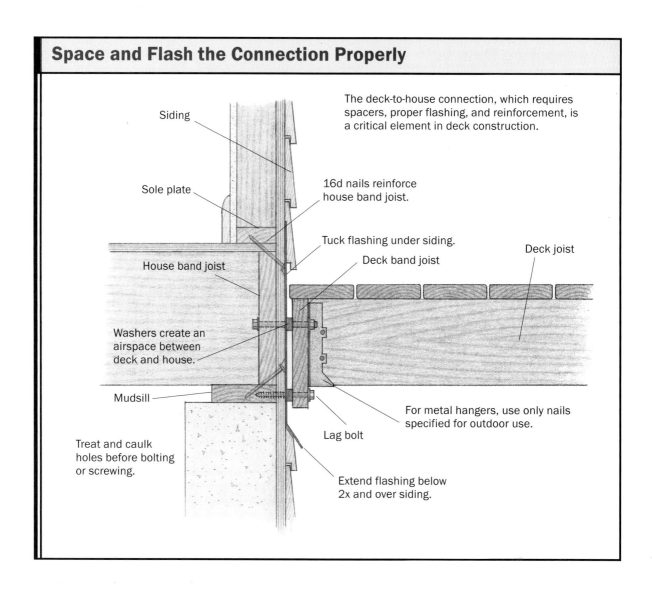

Siding

Sole plate

House band joist

Washers create an airspace between deck and house.

Mudsill

Treat and caulk holes before bolting or screwing.

The deck-to-house connection, which requires spacers, proper flashing, and reinforcement, is a critical element in deck construction.

16d nails reinforce house band joist.

Tuck flashing under siding.

Deck band joist

Deck joist

Lag bolt

For metal hangers, use only nails specified for outdoor use.

Extend flashing below 2x and over siding.

Proper Size and Spacing of Fasteners Are Critical

Wherever you use bolts in a deck, the strength of the connection depends on the correct size and spacing of the fasteners.

To attach decks to the band joist of a house, where you use 12-in., 16-in. or 24-in. joist spacing, two ⅜-in.-dia. lag screws are needed every 24 in. for a 6-ft. span. Two ½-in.-dia. lag screws are needed every 24 in. for spans of 6 ft. to 16 ft.

joist of the house before installing screws or bolts. It's also prudent to add spacers, such as a few washers, between the two structures to allow the gap between the deck and the house to dry. You also should extend metal flashing under the siding above the deck and over the siding below the deck.

If the deck is attached to the house, it may be necessary to reinforce the band joist of the house to resist lateral forces that tend to pull the deck from the house. Drive 16d nails at 8 in. o.c. through the sole plates and mudsills, from above and from below, to add support to the band joist in new construction.

It may also help to provide additional bracing on the deck; however, our recommendation to reinforce the band joist highlights the need to transfer the deck loads adequately to the house framing. There have been cases where the deck was firmly attached to the band joist, but the band joist was not secured to resist the deck loads and was ripped from the house when the deck failed. Of course, we recommend X-bracing between the posts for freestanding decks. This topic is covered in our deck manual in more detail (*Wood Decks: Materials, Construction, and Finishing,* published by the Forest Products Society, 608-231-1361 or www.forestprod.org).

Don't Skimp on Fasteners

The two most important things to remember when choosing deck fasteners—framing nails, decking nails, screws, joist hangers, bolts, and lags—are their holding capacity and their resistance to corrosion. Inadequate fasteners or improperly installed fasteners can cause connections to loosen, and when they corrode, they weaken the surrounding wood.

Most fasteners are made of mild steel or stainless steel and are produced in a variety of styles. Protective coatings are often applied to mild steel fasteners. Stainless-steel fasteners last the longest, followed by hot-dipped galvanized-steel fasteners. There are newer types of fastener coatings on the market, but we haven't extensively evaluated their longevity.

It's important to remember that aluminum fasteners can be used for fastening untreated wood but that aluminum can rapidly corrode in wood treated with preservatives containing copper.

Use Heavy-Coated Galvanized Fasteners

Galvanized coatings protect the steel underneath, so when the coating is gone, the underlying steel corrodes. That makes the thickness of this protective coating critical.

To galvanize fasteners, manufacturers apply coatings of zinc, cadmium, or zinc/cadmium by electroplating, mechanical plating, chemically treating, or hot dipping (dunking the fastener in molten zinc). The thickness of these coatings varies significantly; hot-dipped coatings are typically the

> *Aluminum fasteners can be used for fastening untreated wood, but aluminum can rapidly corrode in wood treated with preservatives containing copper.*

Stainless Steel Is a Bargain

Stainless-steel nails, bolts, and screws can cost many times what conventional fasteners cost; but considering the overall investment of lumber and time put into a deck, they're worth the price, especially in wet or salty environments. Our research shows that even after years of severe exposure, stainless steel holds up well.

The problem with stainless steel is that the metal is softer and more difficult to drive than carbon steel, which may result in more waste from bent nails or damaged screw heads.

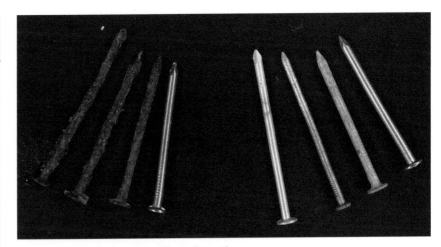

Stainless steel lasts longer. The nails on the right side of each pair were nailed into solid-wood blocks and subjected to 14 years of exposure to high humidity. From left, stainless steel, hot-dipped galvanized, mechanically galvanized, and electroplated galvanized.

thickest and, in our experience, give the best corrosion resistance.

Unfortunately, many builders use electroplated nails for outdoor construction because they are available for use in nail guns. Our research found that electroplated nails don't last as long as hot-dipped galvanized nails.

In addition to nails, there are lots of hangers, post supports, hidden deck-board fasteners, and other metal hardware available for use in deck construction. Just as with nails, screws, and bolts, metal deck hardware should have a thick, durable, protective coating.

Avoid Smooth-Shank Nails, and Avoid Nail Pop-up

After years of getting wet and drying out, smooth-shank box and common nails can lose their withdrawal resistance, pop up, and loosen connections—especially if they're used to secure deck boards. So for deck boards, we recommend deformed-shank nails, such as spiral-groove and ring-shank nails, or screws.

These deformed-shank nails resist withdrawal effects from cupping and from wetting and drying cycles. Pop-up can also occur

Ring-shank Nails Won't Do This.

After years of moisture cycling, smooth-shank nails work loose and pop up. Deformed-shank nails stay put.

when nails are too short. We recommend the use of at least 3-in.-long nails (10d) to secure 1-in.-thick deck boards and 3½-in.-long nails (16d) for thicker deck boards.

Screws—especially drywall type or bugle-head "multipurpose" screws—seem to have found a niche in deck building, too. Like other metal fasteners, screws used outside must be able to withstand the wetting and drying cycles that can cause weakening of metal and loosening of connections. Screws have advantages over nails: They are effective in drawing down cupped or twisted decking, and they can be removed. For screws, the length recommendations given previously apply. A word of warning about multipurpose screws, however: They are not intended to fasten joist hangers. Use only manufacturer-specified hanger nails to attach joist hangers.

Use Lag Screws Where Bolts Can't Go

For fastening a 2x to a thicker member where a through bolt won't work, lag screws work well. Just remember that pilot holes should be 60% to 70% of the diameter of the threaded portion of the screw. Therefore, a ⅜-in.-dia. lag screw would get a ¼-in. pilot hole for the threaded portion, followed by a ⅜-in.-pilot hole for the unthreaded portion.

Lag screws need to be long enough so that at least half of their length penetrates the thicker member. A flat washer should be used under the head, but not tightened so much that it crushes the wood.

Bolts are more rigid and typically stronger than lag screws. Remember to drill the pilot hole no more than ⅟₁₆ in. larger in diameter than the bolt. It's best to use flat washers under both the bolt head and the nut to distribute the force over a larger area and reduce crushing of the wood.

It's also a good idea to saturate pilot holes with wood preservative or a water-repellent preservative (such as Woodguard®, Daps Woodlife, or Cuprinol®). Water can collect around fasteners and promote decay. Check lag screws and bolts periodically for tightness.

We haven't tested many of the newer fasteners, such as hidden fasteners, so we have no data. However, the use of hidden hardware may make it more difficult to replace a problem deck board should the need arise. On the plus side, these products don't puncture the top of the deck board with a fastener, eliminating a site for water collection and corrosion.

Give Your Deck a Proper Finish

A lot of time and money goes into building a deck. To keep it looking good and to ensure that it lasts, the deck needs a good finish. Unless you apply a finish, discoloration, checking, and permanent damage can occur even with preservative-treated wood.

In general, wood finishes fall into two categories: those that form a film and don't penetrate the wood, and those that don't form a film and penetrate the wood. After a great deal of research, we recommend penetrating finishes.

Film-forming finishes include paints of all descriptions, solid-color stains, varnishes and lacquers. Penetrating finishes include solvent-borne, oil-based water repellents, water-repellent preservatives, and oil-based semitransparent stains. Film-forming finishes usually lead to failure because the film can't tolerate the moisture cycling of deck lumber. Once the film is cracked, water gets under it, and the finish blisters and peels.

Choose a Finish That Really Soaks In

Water repellents and water-repellent preservative pretreatments penetrate to protect wood. These products contain a moisture inhibitor, such as paraffin wax, and a binder—but not necessarily pigment. The amount of water repellent in the mixture varies among

Paints, varnishes, and other finishes that form solid films are bad for use on decks because of exposure to sunlight and moisture cycling.

The difference between film-forming and penetrating finishes is clear. The finish on the left is latex paint, which forms a film and isn't recommended for decks. In the middle is a penetrating water-repellent stain, and on the right is a penetrating water repellent; both are good on decks.

brands. A low concentration of repellent is about 1%, so it can be used as a pretreatment. Others have a high concentration of water repellent—about 3%—and are standalone finishes. If the label says "paintable," the finish probably contains the lower concentration of water repellent.

The difference between a water repellent and a water-repellent preservative is that the preservative contains a mildewcide. The use of a mildewcide even in a finish applied to preservative-treated wood is recommended because the wood preservative doesn't resist mildew.

Water-repellent preservatives also are available in forms that contain nondrying oil solvents such as paraffin oil. These products penetrate the wood but don't dry inside the wood.

Several commercial wood treaters are marketing 5/4-in. radius-edge decking that has a dual treatment of water repellent and preservative. Although this process is relatively new and its long-term performance isn't well established, we believe these products are worth the extra cost.

Generally, dual treatments are used on #1 grade lumber rather than #2, which is a more common grade for treated lumber. Therefore, some of the increase in price reflects the use of this better-quality wood.

Finally, we believe that the use of water repellents and water-repellent preservatives does increase the life of fasteners; however, we have never quantified this. We have found that these treatments can decrease iron staining if poor-quality fasteners are used.

Don't Overapply Stain Finishes

Semitransparent oil-based stain finishes penetrate wood, provide color, and often contain water repellents or water-repellent preservatives. Some manufacturers make semitransparent decking stains, which have enhanced water repellency and better wearing resistance. Don't confuse decking stains with siding stains, which aren't for use on horizontal wearing surfaces. If you apply too many coats of stain, a film will form on the wood, and it will eventually crack and cause problems. If applied properly, semitransparent oil-based stains penetrate into the wood without forming a film.

Semitransparent deck stains last much longer than clear water-repellent preservatives because the pigment protects both the wood and the preservative from the damaging effects of the sun. One problem with stains is that the stain may wear off in high-traffic areas such as steps, and it may be difficult to hide these patterns completely when restaining.

More than one coat of semitransparent oil-based stain can be applied as long as subsequent coats are applied while the first is still wet and as long as not so much is applied that a film forms on the surface.

Preservative-Treated Wood Shouldn't Affect the Finish

Waterborne preservative treatments don't affect the finishing characteristics of wood and may enhance the durability of some semitransparent stains. Some preservatives contain chromium oxides that bond to the wood, decreasing degradation of the surface, and increasing the durability of semitransparent stains, often by a factor of two to three.

Other common wood preservatives don't contain chromium oxides, so staining this type of treated lumber is similar to staining untreated wood. Two nonchromium treatments are ammoniacal copper zinc arsenate (ACZA) and ammoniacal copper quaternary (ACQ).

Don't Put Off Applying the Finish

On a newly built deck, apply the finish after the wood dries below about 20% moisture content. If your lumber is not preservative treated and is grade stamped S-DRY (surface dry), KD (kiln dried), or MC-15 (average moisture content 15%) or is treated and stamped KDAT (kiln dried after treatment), it can be finished immediately. If treated and stamped S-DRY, KD, or MC-15, the wood was dried only before treatment. Ideally, these boards should be finished before installation so that the end grain of each board can be coated.

It's often recommended to wait a year to finish a deck. We think a year is too long to wait because checking, cracking, and splintering can occur. We don't think you should wait more than two months to apply finish to your deck.

Brushing on the finish is best, but follow the manufacturer's recommendations. You can apply the finish faster if one person sprays and another person follows and works the finish into the wood with a brush.

To avoid lap marks in semitransparent stains, brush the stain on only two or three boards at a time and stain along their full length. Second coats of semitransparent stains should be applied while the first coat is still wet (within 30 minutes to 45 minutes), or they won't absorb. If the first coat is dry, it seals the surface, and the second coat forms a film.

To maintain the water-repellent finish of your deck, it's best to reapply a finish annually or semiannually. The most obvious way to tell if your deck needs refinishing is to see if water beads on the surface or is absorbed. If water beads, there is no need to refinish. If it doesn't, apply a water repellent. If mildew is a problem, refinish with a water-repellent preservative. Usually, water repellents and water-repellent preservatives can be applied over existing finishes; however, it's always a good idea to test compatibility in an inconspicuous area.

If you refinish a deck finished with a semitransparent stain, be careful not to build up too much finish. Wait long enough that pigment loss is evident, or apply a clear water repellent or water-repellent preservative over the existing semitransparent stain for extra water repellency.

Bob Falk, P. E., is a structural engineer and Sam Williams is a chemist at the USDA Forest Products Laboratory in Madison, Wisconsin. Their colleagues Andy Baker and Mark Knaebe contributed to this article. Falk and Williams are co-authors of a handbook on wood decks, Wood Decks: Materials, Construction, and Finishing.

To maintain the water-repellent finish of your deck, it's best to reapply a finish annually or semiannually.

Sources

Forest Products Society
2801 Marshall Ct.
Madison, WI 53705
(608) 231-1361
www.forestprod.org-
Wood Decks: Materials, Construction, and Finishing

Getting a Deck Off to a Good Start

■ BY PETER J. BILODEAU

Building a square, level deck with all its support posts landing dead on their intended footings is Carpentry 101. But a quick survey of local job sites makes me think that some carpenters skipped that course.

The most obvious problem I see is posts that almost miss their supporting piers. If only part of the post lands on the pier, the deck isn't supported as designed. And even if a misfit doesn't create a structural problem, it looks cobbled together.

Out-of-square decks can be more of a problem for carpenters than for home owners. Miters in the railings won't be at 45°, and joints in the deck boards won't land squarely on the joists. These flaws can be worked around, but they shouldn't have to be. Besides, squaring up a deck is easier than fine-tuning a bunch of miter joints.

When decks are built out of level, it's either because the carpenters screwed up or because they wanted the deck to slope away from the house to allow water runoff. But I like decks to be level because the railings look better. Newels installed on a sloping deck may not look plumb, even when they're dead perfect, because they don't meet the deck at 90°.

What about water runoff? Most decks are built so that the decking runs parallel to the house. Water runs the width of a board, then drips between the deck boards to the ground. On a level deck, some small amount of water may follow the bottom of the joist toward the house, but my detailing of the rim joist ensures that it won't get as far as the wall.

There isn't room here to detail the entire process of building decks. Instead, I'll explain how I frame the perimeter level and square and how I land the posts perfectly on their piers. A well-begun deck is a deck that's easy to finish well.

Set the Deck below the Floor of the House

I step the deck down, usually 6½ in., from the threshold of any door leading onto it (top photo, p. 84). If a door is level with the deck, it's difficult to keep rain or melting snow from running under the door and ruining the floor of the house. Also, if the deck is

Frame the Deck's Perimeter Square and Level First

This provides a ready reference for laying out the footings so that the support posts land perfectly on their footings. This method is very helpful on steep or uneven ground.

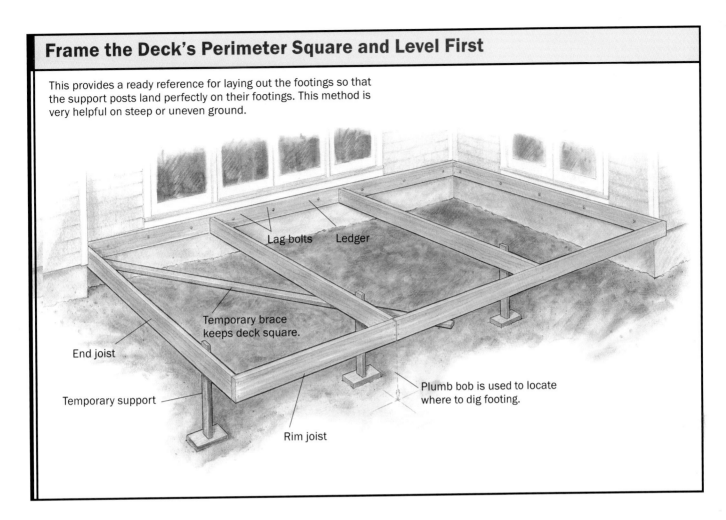

Lag bolts

Ledger

Temporary brace keeps deck square.

End joist

Temporary support

Rim joist

Plumb bob is used to locate where to dig footing.

level with the house floor, the threshold may present more of a trip hazard. With an obvious step, however, people are more likely to notice this change in floor level.

The houses I build are normally sided with cedar, a rot-resistant wood. I've had good success installing a pressure-treated ledger, typically a 2x8, directly over the siding. I nail ⅜-in. by 1½-in. pressure-treated shims on 16-in. centers to the back of the ledger before securing it to the house (top left photo, p. 84) to make a space for water to drain.

Because most of the decks I build are on houses I've built, I'm certain the bottom course of siding is level. So I measure up from there and snap a chalkline that establishes the top of the ledger. If I'm unsure about whether siding is level over the width of a deck, I check the level with a transit.

After cutting the ledger to length, I nail it to the house with 16d galvanized nails. I use

Siding behind Ledger Substitutes for Flashing

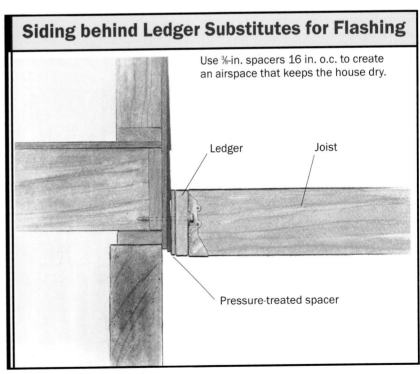

Use ⅜-in. spacers 16 in. o.c. to create an airspace that keeps the house dry.

Ledger

Joist

Pressure-treated spacer

Locate the deck lower than the house floor. Creating a step from the deck into the house helps keep rainwater from getting under the threshold.

The author applies the ledger directly over the siding. Strips nailed to the back of the ledger create an airspace allowing water to drain.

The author lays out joist locations before lag-bolting the ledger to the house so that joists won't fall atop the bolts.

The end and center joists are propped level to support the rim joist. Because these joists hang from the ledger, which also is level, they establish the entire deck as a level plane.

only enough nails to keep the ledger from falling off until I lag-bolt it home. Before drilling the ledger for lags, I lay out the joist spacing. Then I drill and screw in a ⅜-in. by 6-in. galvanized lag and washer every 16 in. between the joist layout and about 3 in. from the top of the ledger (bottom left photo). On houses with 12-in. joists, this layout puts the lags safely into the rim joist. If the house has 10-in. joists, I lower the lags about 1 in. and drive them into the mudsill.

Frame the Perimeter before You Pour the Piers

I cut and install the two end joists next. The deck featured in this article fits into an alcove between two wings of a house, so leveling the first end joist was simple. I butted it to the ledger, had my helper watch the level, and nailed the joist to the house.

The second end joist was more typical because the wing of the house alongside it was only about 2 ft. long. I tacked one end to the ledger, and with my helper reading the level, I nailed a temporary leg near the end of the joist. I complete the end joist's attachment to the ledger by using Simpson Strong-Tie® L70 angle connectors.

Next, I nail the rim joist to the end joists. This deck was longer than the stock I had for the rim joist. Therefore, I installed a joist in the middle of the deck, supported level with a temporary leg, to join the two pieces of the rim joist together (right photo, facing page). I located this joist so that the joint would be above a footing and a post.

I cut the rim-joist pieces to length and nail them to the two end joists and to the center joist (photo right). Now the deck's perimeter and height are established. After the posts are set, the rim joist will be doubled, and the joists will be attached to it with joist hangers.

At this point, I square up the deck by measuring diagonally from corner to corner (center photo). I push the rim joist one way or the other until the measurements are equal, then brace the deck square by nailing a long 2x4 diagonally below the joists (bottom photo). I nail the brace below the joists so that it won't interfere with joisting and decking.

Nail the rim joist to the end and middle joists. A second rim joist will go on after the posts are up, strengthening the assembly to support the joists.

Squaring the deck requires a long tape and a helper. The rim joist is adjusted until the deck's diagonals are equal.

A 2x4 nailed diagonally under the joists holds the deck square.

Use a Plumb Bob to Locate the Piers

After the deck is square, I locate and dig the holes for the footings. Their spacing depends on the size of the deck, but 6 ft. apart is typical. I extend the support posts above the deck to serve as newels. This spacing provides good support for the railings, too.

Stretching a tape along the rim joist, I mark the post centers on its back and drop a plumb bob to locate the footing centers. With stakes driven into the ground, I mark the centers where the footings will go.

The depth of the holes has to be below the frost line. Here on Cape Cod, that means 42 in., but you should check local codes. If the holes are dug in a finished lawn, I shovel soil onto plywood or a tarp to ease cleanup.

I make the holes fairly wide, about 2 ft. in diameter, because the footing needs a big footprint to spread out the load from a deck (top photo, left). Once the holes are dug, I mix bagged gravel-mix concrete in a wheelbarrow. I pour 8 in. of concrete in each hole and smooth it with a scrap of wood.

Cape Cod is generally blessed with a firm, sandy soil that is easily dug yet doesn't cave in. Digging footing holes here is easy enough that the deck framing doesn't really interfere. If you live someplace where digging is difficult, though, you may want to

An 8-in.-thick concrete footing will support the deck. To ensure precise positioning, the hole is located with a plumb bob and dug after the rim joist is nailed on.

A 12-in. Sonotube rests on the footing and brings the concrete to grade. The plumb bob is a reference to keep the Sonotube plumb and centered during backfill.

This anchor resists uplift and allows the post to be tweaked plumb before the nut is tightened.

attach the rim joist temporarily to lay out the footings, then remove it to dig.

Backfill around the Sonotubes

Once the concrete is firm enough that backfilling the hole won't contaminate the concrete with soil, I get my plumb bob. Because the stakes locating the footing centers were removed to dig the holes, I have to plumb down again from the rim joist to mark the centers of the footings. With the centers marked on the footings, I position the Sonotubes®, tubular cardboard forms, that form the piers to grade (bottom photo, left).

I use 12-in. Sonotubes under 4x6 posts. Occasionally, I'll use 10-in. Sonotubes if 4x4 posts are to be used. These sizes leave plenty of room for the post and its anchor to sit comfortably on the concrete.

Measuring from the footings to 1 in. above finished grade tells me the height of the Sonotubes. After cutting one to length, I center a Sonotube on its footing and backfill. I hang the plumb bob over the center of the Sonotube when backfilling; this way, keeping the pier plumb is easy. Keep in mind that the Sonotube doesn't have to be exactly in the middle of the footing, just fairly close. Then I fill the Sonotube with concrete mix and smooth the top with a trowel.

Taller Decks Need Secure Anchoring

If the deck is to be 24 in. or higher off the ground and in a windy spot, wind lift is a concern. In these cases, I fasten posts to concrete with Simpson Strong-Tie AB46 post bases (bottom photo). These post bases affix to the concrete with ½-in. by 6-in. galvanized foundation anchor bolts placed in the centers of the piers (top left photo, facing page). Just ¾ in. of anchor bolt sticks out.

For lower decks, I set the post on an aluminum post foot such as the Simpson

If uplift is unlikely, cheaper hardware anchors the posts. A cast-aluminum base keeps the post off the ground.

After placing the concrete, the plumb bob is again used to mark the center. Depending on the anchoring hardware, a dot marks the spot for a bolt or is simply a reference for setting the post.

Plumb, level, and on the footing. Notched to support the rim joist, this 4x6 post continues above the deck and will eventually support the railing.

Strong-Tie AP series (top right photo). The post foot elevates the post base above the concrete, reducing the chance of rot. (Even pressure-treated wood can rot; sometimes the preservatives don't reach the centers of larger timbers. Cutting into the center of a board often exposes untreated wood.)

When using post feet, I anchor each post to the concrete with two 2-in. by ¾-in. galvanized angle brackets. The brackets are held to the concrete with ¼-in. by 2-in. expanding masonry anchors and to the posts with 16d galvanized nails.

Determine the Post Height

Setting the posts—actually connecting the deck to its footings—is the final step in laying out a deck. I check that the end and rim joists haven't dropped out of level and adjust the temporary legs to level the joists if necessary. Once the perimeter of the deck is level, I place the anchoring hardware on the concrete and measure from the hardware to the bottom of the rim joist.

I mark the height on the posts and notch them to fit around the rim joist. Corner posts are notched to receive the end joists as

well as the rim joist. Because the end joists are single members, this notch is only 1½ in. deep. If railings are needed, I cut the 4x6s now to accommodate the required railing height. Two ½-in. carriage bolts hold each post to the rim.

Now the deck is ready for joists, decking, and rails. It is level and square, and the posts fall exactly on their footings.

Peter J. Bilodeau is a builder from Osterville, Massachusetts.

Sources

Simpson Strong-Tie
2600 International St.
Columbus, OH 43228
(800) 999-5099
www.strongtie.com

The Care and Feeding of Wooden Decks

■ BY JON TOBEY

The Eskimos have five dozen words for snow. Here in the waterlogged Pacific Northwest, weather forecasters have an equally diverse vocabulary whether they're calling for light rain, showers, isolated storms, sprinkles, drizzle, mist, driving rain, or mizzle. If you live here, you can expect to get wet nearly every day from September through June. I can't imagine a less hospitable place to build a wooden deck. But to the average Seattle homeowner, a house with less than half the yard covered by cascading decks is unfinished.

I'd be happier if everyone built stone patios. But homeowners depend on me to make sure their decks aren't reduced to a heap of compost. Fortunately, I can assure them that with modern technology and periodic maintenance, a deck can enjoy a long, productive life.

Penetrating Finishes Are Better Than Paints

Materials for wooden decks vary from region to region, but none of them is maintenance free. I use the same procedures for all wooden decks. When homeowners ask me beforehand how to finish a new deck, I caution against paint or solid stain. Any horizontal surface, especially one subjected to foot traffic, is extremely difficult to keep paint on. Even solid alkyd stains, which for years have been recommended for decks, are too brittle and merely sit on top of the wood (like paint), awaiting the opportunity to peel off.

I prefer penetrating finishes. Properly applied penetrating finishes, such as semi-transparent alkyd stains and clear wood preservatives, are absorbed into the wood fibers to protect better against mold, mildew, rot, and UV degradation. Penetrating finishes are also easier to recoat because over time, they fade rather than flake.

The best penetrating finish I've found is Clear Wood Finish UV® from The Flood Co., which enhances the wood's natural beauty but can also be tinted like a stain. CWF is an emulsified oil, so it cleans up like a latex but offers the protection of a petroleum product. I have found it far superior to the more popular paraffin-based coatings (such as Thompson's Water Seal®) that require biannual retreatment to be effective. Even with the best

> *Materials for wooden decks vary from region to region, but none of them is maintenance free.*

finishes, however, the surface of the deck needs to be recoated every three years to provide maximum protection for the wood.

Cleaning and Pressure-washing Come First

Unless they've been painted, I treat older decks basically the same as new ones. Every deck gets a thorough broom cleaning; while I'm sweeping an older deck, I check for damaged spots and mark any boards that need to be replaced. After all the leaves and dog hair have been swept away, I spray on a specially formulated deck cleaner, such as Cuprinol Revive® or Simple Wash from Biowash. Applied full strength with a garden sprayer (photo bottom left), the deck cleaner kills mold and mildew and cuts through dirt and oxidation. It also removes mill glazing from new decks, which means you don't have to let new lumber "silver" for a year before applying a finish. The deck cleaner works almost immediately, so as soon as I'm finished spraying it on, I return to the starting point and begin a light pressure-washing.

A lot of people are afraid of using a pressure washer on a deck, and with good reason. Used improperly, a pressure washer can do more harm than good. In the right hands, however, a pressure washer prepares a

deck for refinishing quickly and effectively. For cleaning decks, I use a 9-hp, 2500-psi machine with a 158 spray tip (158 is the angle formed by the fan of water as it shoots from the tip).

To avoid wasted motion, I spray a 6-ft.-wide swath, then overlap the next swath by 12 in. to 18 in. to make sure that the edges blend together. For maximum cleaning power with minimal abrasion, I hold the spray tip 6 in. to 9 in. above the surface of the deck and sweep the wand over the boards in a flattened pendulum motion, lifting the wand away from the deck at the end of one pass and lowering it gradually back at the beginning of the next.

When I'm able to wiggle underneath the deck, I give the underside a quick pressure wash as well. I usually don't find much mold or mildew, which would require an intensive wash; mostly I'm just concerned with cleaning out spider webs, splashed mud and other debris. It's a dirty job, but somebody really ought to do it. After I wash the underside, the top gets another quick rinse.

Preparing the Railings

While I'm spraying the deck, I also pressure-wash both sides of the railings. For the most effective cleaning, I keep the fan of water as perpendicular to the vertical surfaces as I

Applied using a garden sprayer, a specially formulated deck cleaner dissolves dirt and oxidation and kills mold and mildew on contact.

For maximum cleaning with minimal abrasion, the author holds the 158 spray tip 6 in. to 9 in. above the deck and gradually sweeps across the boards in a flattened pendulum motion.

Dealing with Paint

Painting a deck is a bad idea to begin with; so whenever a painted deck needs to be refinished, I prefer to remove the paint and start over with bare wood. Unlike most paint removal, stripping paint from the surface of a deck is incredibly easy, thanks to a product called Stripex® from Wood Care Systems™.

After donning heavy rubber gloves and oversize rubber boots, I use an acid brush to swab the stripper over the surface of the deck. When that's done, all it takes is a gentle rinse with a pressure washer, and the paint is history. Unlike some paint strippers that must be rinsed with a neutralizer, Stripex is water-neutralized, so no additional step is required after the product is washed off. One advantage to this process is that instead of being covered with plastic, nearby plants can be merely wetted down with water for protection during application. Don't let the ease of its use fool you, however. Stripex is a powerful base that can inflict serious burns on unprotected skin. I have the scars to prove it.

Although it's easy to strip the surface of a deck, it's much harder to strip painted railings completely, so I concentrate on problem areas such as the top of the handrail and anyplace else where the paint is flaking off. If the handrail is peeling badly, I use a mechanical paint scraper to get down to bare wood quickly. I use hand scrapers to remove loose paint elsewhere on the railing; then all the surfaces get a light going-over with a palm sander loaded with 80-grit sandpaper. I also make sure to recaulk all the joints.

Although I prefer to use a penetrating finish on a deck, whenever I've had to cover a solid finish (paint or stain), I've gotten

Stripper is applied with bucket and brush.

Pressure-washing removes paint and neutralizes stripper.

good results using Sherwin-Williams® Woodscapes® Solid Latex Stain. This stain can be tinted to match any house color; in the past four years, I have used it over bare wood, solid stain, and paint without any failures.

Quick Fix for Support Posts

With so much end grain exposed to the elements, uncapped support posts are always a problem. If the design permits, I simply cut back the posts to solid wood, then install inexpensive but good-looking copper caps, which are available at any hardware store.

can. At the same time, I also direct the spray deep into the crevices to drive out all the bugs and gunk that have taken up residence.

After washing the deck, I give the railing assembly the once-over, checking for signs of rot. I pay attention to the top of the handrail, especially if it has exposed fasteners, and to the end grain at the top of uncapped support posts. If I find any rotten spots, I use liquid borates to kill the rot organism; then, after it has been allowed to dry, I use epoxy to repair the damage.

Brightening Follows Cleaning

Preparing a deck for finish actually involves two chemical treatments. A side effect of the cleaning stage is that it leaves even brand new decks looking tired and gray. But that's just temporary. As soon as I finish pressure-washing, I fill up the garden sprayer with Deckmaster Wood Brightener and spray a liberal coating over all the bare wood. This oxalic acid–based product quickly restores wood darkened by age or chemicals to a like-new appearance. I usually let the brightener soak into the wood for 20 minutes or so, and then rinse the deck lightly with the pressure washer.

Penetrating finish won't soak in unless the wood is dry, so after I'm done swabbing the deck, I allow it to dry for a minimum of three warm, rain-free days before I apply the finish. During the interim, I usually move on to another job, but before I leave, I replace the boards that I previously determined were too rotten to save. To make the new boards blend in, I pick a semitransparent stain from my collection that closely matches the color of the weathered deck boards. By the time the stain wears away, the new board will be almost unnoticeable.

After the cleaning process has left these old deck boards looking their age, an oxalic acid–based wood brightener quickly restores their youthful sparkle. The brightener is allowed to stand for 20 minutes, and then is rinsed off with the pressure washer.

Sprayed Finish Gets Nooks and Crannies

There's no reason you can't finish a deck using brushes and rollers, but it's much faster to use spray equipment. You can also get better coverage using a sprayer because it enables you to force the coating into tight spots that would be difficult or impossible to reach with a brush. Spray equipment is expensive to buy, but compared with the cost of labor, it's cheap to rent. Sprayers and pressure washers are offered for rent at many paint-supply houses as well as at most rental centers.

With a brush, I'd start outside the deck on the tops of the railings and work my way down to the deck, and then in toward the house. Spraying is tougher because I have to use masking to control overspray.

Which Comes First, Deck or Railings?

When all the surfaces are getting the same finish, I generally spray both sides of the railings and leave the deck boards for last. If the railings are getting a different finish than the deck surface (as was the case on this job), I have to spray the deck first.

On this job, the railings were originally painted to match the trim of the house. Stripping all the paint would have cost a fortune, so I'd previously scraped and sanded the loose spots. When the deck finish is dry, the railings get a fresh coat of stain.

Using an airless paint sprayer with a #617 spray tip, I apply the CWF coating, moving lengthwise along the deck boards from one end of the deck to the other (photo top right). I hold the spray gun 12 in. to 18 in. from the surface and move just fast enough to put down an even, wet coat. After every couple of passes, I put down the spray gun and roll the finish using a ½-in.-nap, 9-in. wide paint roller (photo bottom right). After rolling, the deck boards should have an even, glossy sheen. If the penetrating finish

The author uses a spray gun to force preservative into every nook and cranny. A 4-ft.-wide painting shield makes sure the finish goes only where it's supposed to go.

To ensure an even application, the finish is rolled after every two or three passes.

soaks in completely, as it often does on thirsty, weathered boards, I spray another light coat before moving on to the next section. When I'm spraying alongside the house or the railings, I use a 4-ft.-wide painting shield to control the overspray.

After the top of the deck has been coated, I crawl underneath, if it's accessible, and soak the bottom of the boards, the joists, the beams, whatever I can get. In my experience, treating the underside of a deck even once can double its life span.

The author covers the deck with tarps, wraps the first floor of the house with plastic sheeting and masks the outside of the railing. After coating the inside of the railing, he'll remove the paper and spray the outside.

Using the painting shield to catch overspray, the author coats the handrail in long, smooth, horizontal strokes.

After painting the handrails, he comes back and coats each side of each baluster in a separate vertical stroke. After every couple of passes, all surfaces are brushed with a disposable painting pad.

Mask Carefully before Spraying the Railings

The downside to spraying the deck first is that I have to let it dry for 24 hours to 72 hours (depending on humidity) before I can finish the railings. When the deck is dry enough to walk on without leaving footprints, I start masking off the surfaces I don't want painted. To protect the house from overspray, I wrap the first floor with a 9-ft.-wide strip of plastic sheeting. I spread clean painter's tarps and masking paper over the deck surface and then run a strip of 3-ft.-wide kraft paper around the outside of the balusters.

These railings were painted, so after removing the loose paint, I applied a coat of Sherwin-Williams Woodscapes Solid Latex

Stain. To spray the railings, I switch to a narrower (#213) spray tip, which puts out a more compact, directional spray fan than the tip I use for the deck boards. I start on one of the inside corners and work counterclockwise, spraying the handrail in long, horizontal strokes (photo above), and the balusters in vertical strokes (photo left). Keeping the spray tip about 12 in. away from the railing, I cover the balusters on three sides and also try to coat as much of the underside of the railing as possible. At the end of each pass with the spray gun, I brush the finish using a disposable painting pad (if I'd been applying a penetrating finish, I would have used a lamb's wool mitt).

Once the railing's interior surface is dry to the touch (on a warm day, usually an hour or less), I remove the kraft paper and spray the outer surfaces of the balusters, as well as any other spots I wasn't able to reach from the inside. I don't need to rehang the paper on the inside because all the vulnerable surfaces are already covered. As soon as I finish this application, the rest of the masking is pulled, a few small touch-ups are made with the disposable pad, and I am done. Unless homeowners really like having me around, I urge them to sweep the deck frequently and to wash it lightly once a year.

Jon Tobey is a painting contractor in Monroe, Washington.

Avoiding Deck Problems

Unfortunately, cleaning and refinishing a deck are not cure-alls. A lot of the problems I see with decks stem from the original construction and landscaping. By far the worst problem is improper flashing where the deck's rim joist is attached to the house. This critical detail must be carefully designed, or the house as well as the deck will suffer.

Another common problem is placing the deck too close to the ground (photo bottom right). The proximity of the moist earth encourages rot to thrive as evaporation pulls moisture directly into the bottom of the deck. I like to see at least 1 ft. of airspace between the bottom of the joists and the ground. If a deck must be built closer to the ground, I recommend providing special drainage beneath the deck and then dipping all of the lumber in preservative before installation.

Fasteners can also be a problem. Deeply countersunk screws or air nails create hundreds of tiny Petri dishes for rot to thrive in. Builders should try to set their fasteners flush with the deck surface (or you can try one of the concealed-fastening systems that are now available). In my experience, however, even deep pockets aren't a problem as long as the deck is regularly cleaned and recoated.

Railings are always a problem, especially when the handrails are made of wide, flat boards. Wide, flat surfaces are great places to set potted plants or to rest drinks, but they're also great places for water to collect, which eventually causes cupping, checking and rot. To reduce cupping, the handrail needs to be relatively thick for its width; a 2x6 is far preferable to a 1x6. If the homeowners will stand for it, the top of the handrail should be beveled to shed water. To prevent cupping further, the handrail should be installed so that the annular rings curve down.

Plants and Decks Don't Mix

Deck boards need air circulation to keep them healthy.
1. Don't place immovable potted plants on the deck.
2. Maintain airspace between decks and shrubbery.
3. Don't allow debris to accumulate between deck boards.
4. Place a barrier between mulch and ground-level framing.

Although framed with pressure-treated yellow pine, this deck has skirtboards, railings and deck boards made of Trex, a composite of recycled polyethylene and wood. The flexibility of Trex makes it a good choice for a curved deck.

Building a Curved Deck with Synthetic Decking

■ BY TED PUTNAM

For me, part of the challenge of custom remodeling has been the opportunity to try something new. When I saw the potential to combine an interesting deck design and new materials, I immediately went to my prospective clients, who received the ideas enthusiastically.

From their house near Long Island Sound, my prospective clients had a wonderful view of a salt marsh and the estuary beyond. They also had a small yard and wanted a backyard deck for recreational space.

After several meetings, we drew up a plan for a stacked semicircular deck. The family could watch marsh birds from the top level or sit around a cozy fireplace/barbecue on the lower deck. A grand staircase facing the water, a wraparound bench, and a small side stair completed the basic design.

My clients also wanted a deck that would withstand constant exposure to salt and the weather extremes of New England. Although we would use pressure-treated yellow pine for the framing material, we ruled out pressure-treated decking because it tends to crack and check after a few seasons. Wooden lumber would also have required steam-bending to fit the desired curves. Having had four years of experience building decks with wood-polymer composites, I suggested Trex decking, which fit the bill perfectly.

Pouring Concrete Efficiently

After digging the post holes and a circular footing for the barbecue, we called for concrete. Normally, we mix small batches of concrete for footings from 80-lb. bags. When we need more than a few post holes but less than a foundation, we make a call to the local ready-mix company for a concrete batch truck. Batch trucks are smaller than big mixers and mix concrete on the spot in the strength that we need. We pay for what we use. The normal batch truck can deliver up to 5 yd. It's also quite a bit faster than mixing the stuff by hand.

An Underground Fixture Becomes the Barbecue Base

Before the framing began, we needed to finalize the fireplace/barbecue design. The owners weren't interested in a fancy gas-fired contraption; they just wanted a place where they could build a real fire for sing-alongs, s'mores, or serious cooking. During the design, we planned for a shallow brick pit built on some sort of concrete-base platform. We found the base after some research and a few phone calls: a wire-mesh reinforced concrete tower normally used to house utilities underground. This concrete tube had a 42-in. dia. We brought in a 40-in.-tall section of the utility tower and set it in place, centered on a circular footing 5 ft. in dia. Next, we filled the tower with rubble and concrete; after the deck was finished, a mason laid the firebrick inside the barbecue.

Once the concrete had cured, we began setting the support posts and beams. We used pressure-treated 4x4 posts to support doubled pressure-treated 2x8 beams that would run under and perpendicular to the joists. We used galvanized connectors to secure the posts and beams, and after bolting the ledger boards to the house, we bent and attached aluminum flashing over the ledger. We then nailed on the joist hangers,

cut the pressure-treated 2x8 joists and began framing. Because Trex has no structural properties, its manufacturer recommends no greater span than 16 in. o.c. for 5/4x6 bull-nose decking in residential applications. We let the joists run long past the support beams and perimeter outline to prepare for the next step of laying out the circles.

To Frame Curves, Start by Framing a Square

With the joists installed and run long, we tacked a piece of ¾-in. plywood roughly in the center of the joists on the upper deck and located the exact center of our first circle on the plywood. We then drove a nail through one end of a 1x3 into the plywood at the centerpoint, and we cut the 1x3 to the circle's radius after subtracting 1½ in. for the skirtboard, ⅜ in. for the lattice and 1½ in. for the plywood band joist.

We swung the homemade trammel over the tops of the joists and marked the curve with a fine-point felt-tip pen. We drew plumb lines with a framing square and cut the joists 2 in. to 3 in. beyond the line with a chainsaw.

To make the curved blocking that would support the plywood band joist, we used the offcuts and cut them to fit between the joists, flush to the top. After nailing the blocking, we redrew the arc and cut to the line with a circular saw. (After trying to cut straight for years, I found that it was surprisingly easy to cut a curve; it was also much faster than cutting with a jigsaw.) The bottom blocking was traced from the top, cut, and nailed into place at the bottom of the joists (top left photo, p. 100). The joist ends were then trimmed flush using a reciprocating saw.

To make the band joist, we ripped ½-in. pressure-treated CDX plywood into 7½-in. wide strips and laminated three layers together across the joist ends. We clamped one end to the starting point and slowly began to glue, clamp, and nail, using construction

Rather than cut joists to length as they were installed, the author found that it was easier to let them extend beyond the proposed outline, draw the circumference with a trammel, and cut them all at once.

Synthetic Decking: An Alternative to Wood

During the past decade, consumers and manufacturers have expressed a growing interest in recycled building materials, including decking. There are now several types of decking made from recycled plastics and/or wood products, as well as others made from plastics such as vinyl. While by no means inclusive, the list of manufacturers on p. 102 will provide some useful sources. Your local lumberyard should be helpful in finding regional suppliers of these synthetics as well.

Dream Deck (at left), Perma-Poly® (center), and Trex (at right).

TimberTech (left), ChoiceDek (center), Carefree Decking® (right front and center), and Phoenix Plastic Lumber (right rear).

adhesive and 8d galvanized box nails (top right photo, p. 100). We let the ends fall without regard to the joist ends and were generous with the glue; we also were careful to stagger the joints on each layer. After completing the lamination, we used the chainsaw and cut the support beams flush with the plywood. We shared a congratulatory coffee break and set off to tackle the larger lower section.

The lower-deck framing was identical to its upper neighbor with one exception: The curving band joist would run parallel to the framing along one side of the deck and would not be supported by the joists. Rather than fill in the void with short blocks, we nailed a length of pressure-treated 2x8 horizontally to the top of the last joist (bottom photo, p. 100). After scribing and cutting the arc, we traced the arc onto a second piece of pressure-treated 2x8 that would serve as bottom blocking. The plywood band joist secured the blocking, and vice versa.

Cutting the curves with a circular saw is easier than it might seem. After drawing the curves with a 1x3 trammel tacked to the centerpoint and nailing off the blocking, the author cut the outline, setting the blade depth to 1⅝ in. to reduce the chance of binding the blade.

The lower blocking was traced and cut before installation. To provide easier nailing and to reduce splitting, the joist ends were cut off with a reciprocating saw after the blocking was installed. Note the vertical lines plumbed down from the saw kerfs on the tops of the joists.

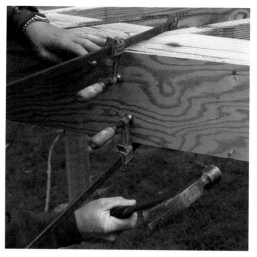

Laminating thinner layers of plywood is an easy wood-bending technique. The author met the challenge of a tightly curved rim joist by laminating three layers of ½-in. pressure-treated plywood onto the joist ends with plenty of construction adhesive, clamps, and careful nailing.

The author had to build in structural blocking where the deck's curve ran parallel to the joists. A 2x8 was nailed to the edge of the last joist, and a 1x3 trammel was used to trace the curve onto the 2x8. After the board was cut, another just like it was nailed to the bottom of the joist, and the two were tied together with a laminated band joist.

through experience that scribe-fitting the decking into the rim yields a more precise joint than installing the decking first. Prebending the 2x10 (top photo, facing page) was a cinch, and in quick succession we attached the skirts with 3½-in. galvanized decking screws into the joists (center photo, facing page). We glued the joints with PVC cement and filled gaps with a mixture of PVC cement and Trex sawdust.

Keep the Decking Straight and Well Supported

It was time to lay the decking down. Because the boards are so flexible, we had to watch closely that the courses didn't wander too much. We snapped a series of chalklines, each representing a double-board width, and screwed a decking board with 2½-in. galvanized decking screws to each chalkline, leaving a board-width space between. We then dropped in another board and centered it by eye, using a scraper or flat bar as needed to match the gaps on both sides.

Bending Reveals the Beauty of Composites

After stapling plastic lattice around the perimeter, we began bending and attaching the 2x10 Trex skirtboard. We used scrap 5/4 decking to establish the height of the skirtboard above the rim; when screwed onto the band joist, the skirt would cover the butt ends of the decking. We've found

On the upper level, the decking ran straight out across the joists, parallel to the house. We scribed and cut the decking to length with a jigsaw, trimming the butt ends with a block plane as needed. The bottom level wasn't so easy. To bring a visual focus to the barbecue, the final design called for the decking to radiate out from the barbecue like spokes in a wheel. This required a significant amount of additional blocking to support the diagonal runs of decking (bottom photo).

Bent Railings Add a Unique Design Element

With the decking complete, we began the railing construction. We predrilled each baluster top and bottom, set the heights, plumbed them up, and screwed the lower ends into the skirtboard.

We prebent the vertical face of the railings by clamping a Trex 2x4 to the inside perimeter of the balusters(top photo, p. 102). After bending, Trex will hold its basic shape for quite a while. We then brought the 2x4 to the top of the balusters, clamped it in place, and screwed it. We tried several different joints to connect the 2x4s, but because of the curved railing, we could not get the joint tight to my complete satisfaction. For future decks, I will special-order longer pieces (Trex can be extruded up to 40 ft. long) and won't have to deal with seams.

The top of the railing was a new challenge. We tried bending a Trex 2x6 on edge but could not get the radius required, so we ripped Trex 2x6s into 1⅜-in. strips. Using PVC cement, we glued and screwed the first strip to the top of the vertical 2x4; this served as our form. We then glued, clamped and screwed the remaining pieces into place (bottom photo, p.102), staggering the seams as we went. Any irregularities were removed with a belt sander.

After completing our work on the railing, we began to build the bench for the lower

Because Trex is made from a composite of recycled high-density polyethylene and wood chips, it has little lateral stiffness and can be bent easily. Once bent, the material keeps its shape for some time without reinforcement.

The skirtboard is screwed to the rim before the decking is laid down. The author preferred to scribe-fit the decking to the skirtboard, which helped maintain precise joints between the butt ends of the decking and the skirt. Scrap decking helped align the skirt as it was clamped and screwed into place.

Composite decking is not structural. The deck design included a segmented section that radiated out from the hub of the barbecue. Because the decking material has poor lateral strength, it must be supported at least every 16 in.

Sources

Carefree Decking
U.S. Plastic Lumber
Corp.
2300 Glades Rd.
Suite 440W
Boca Raton, FL 33431
(561) 394-3511
www.usplasticlumber-.com
Recycled high-density polyethylene

Choice Dek
Advanced Environmental Recycling Technologies Inc.
P.O. Box 116
Junction, TX 76849
(800) 951-5117
www.choicedek.com
High-density polyethylene and cedar composite

Dream Deck
Thermal Industries
301 Brushton Ave.
Pittsburgh, PA 15221
(800) 245-1540
www.thermalindustries-.com
Polyvinyl chloride

Perma-Poly
Renew Plastics
P.O. Box 480
Luxemburg, WI 54217
(800) 666-5207
www.renewplastics.com
Recycled high-density polyethylene

Phoenix Plastic Lumber
Outwater Plastic Industries Inc.
4 Passaic St.
Woodridge, NJ 07075
(888) 688-9283
www.outwater.com
Recycled high-density polyethylene

TimberTech
P.O. Box 182880
Columbus, OH 43218
(800) 307-7780
Wood/plastic resin composite

Trex
160 Exeter Dr.
Winchester, VA 22603
(540) 678-4070
www.trex.com
Recycled wood and polyethylene composite

Balusters screwed to the rim joist serve as a bending form for the railing top. After spacing and securing the lower ends of the balusters, the author used bar clamps to prebend the curve of the 2x4 vertical railing face.

After attempting to edge-bend a Trex 2x6, the author laminated the top part of the T-shaped railing by ripping the Trex into thin strips and reassembling them with PVC cement and screws.

level. We constructed right-angle pressure-treated 2x4 supports and secured one to every fourth baluster and to the deck, providing a finished seat height of 19 in. from the deck. After tying the supports together with a vertical Trex 2x4 as a facing, we ripped, bent, glued, and then screwed 5/4x6 Trex for the bench seat as we had for the railing.

New Materials and Designs Require Time

When I work, I strive to learn new ideas and techniques. Unfortunately, learning new techniques can be time-consuming and expensive. After this experience, I'm ready for the next challenge. Bent glass rails, anyone?

Ted Putnam is the owner of Putnam Custom Carpentry/Deck Creations in Chester, Connecticut.

Railing against the Elements

■ BY SCOTT MCBRIDE

The moist climate of New York's Hudson Valley isn't exactly ideal for carpenters like myself. We have muggy summers, slushy winters, and three months of rain in between. As we struggle through weeks of unremitting precipitation with fogged-up levels and wet chalklines, there is but one consolation: come April, a billion fungal spores will bloom reaching into every water-logged mudsill, fascia, and doorstep. That means a guaranteed crop of rot-repair jobs in the coming season.

Of all the woodwork exposed to the elements, none is so vulnerable as the white pine porch railing. With the right combination of faulty detailing and wind-driven rain, a railing can be reduced to shredded wheat in about eight years. I typically rebuild several of these railings each year. In this article I'll describe one such project.

Getting Organized

A railing around the flat roof of a garage had rotted out and the owner asked me to build a new one. This wasn't a deck that was used, so the railing was decorative rather than functional, and one of my worries was installing

The original railing around the deck over the garage rotted out prematurely, so the owner of the house commissioned a new railing of a slightly different design. Carefully detailed of cypress and cedar, the new railing should last a long time.

Spacing Balusters

Spacing balusters correctly is a simple trick, but it's surprising how many carpenters are stumped by it. The object is to have equal spaces between each baluster and between balusters and posts.

Suppose your railing is 71⅝ in. long, your balusters are 1½ in. sq., and you want a spacing of 4 in. o.c.—that is, 1½ in. of wood, 2½ in. of air, 1½ in. of wood, and so on.

Begin the layout from the post on the left, by tentatively laying off a 2½ in. space ending at point A in the drawing. From there you stretch a tape and see how close you come to the post on the right with a multiple of 4 in. In this case 68 in. (a multiple of 4) brings us to point B, which is 1⅛ in. from the right-hand post. Forget about this remainder for the moment.

Dividing 68 by 4 tells you that you will have 17 intervals containing one baluster and one space, plus the extra space you laid out at the start. That makes 17 balusters and 18 spaces. Now you're going to lay out the combined dimensions of all 17 balusters (17 x 1½ in. = 25½ in.) from the left-hand post. That brings you to point C. From there you're going to lay off the combined dimensions of all the spaces, bringing you to point B—close, but not close enough. To land directly at the post, divide the remaining 1⅛-in. by 18 (the number of spaces) and add the quotient to each space. How fortunate 1⅛ ÷ 18 = 1/16. That gives you a nice, neat adjusted dimension for the space of 2 9/16 in.

If the numbers don't divide evenly, I'll use a pair of spring dividers to find the exact space dimension by trial and error, stepping off the distance from point C to the post. When I find the right setting, I lay off the first space. Then I add this dimension to the baluster width, reset the spring dividers to the sum distance, and step off the actual spacing. This method avoids the accumulated error that happens when using a ruler and pencil, not to mention all that excruciating arithmetic.

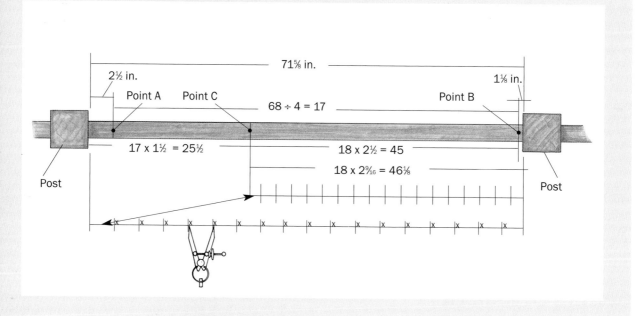

the new railing without making the roof leak (more about that later). On a house across town, my customer had spotted a railing that he liked and asked if I could reproduce it. I said I could and took down the address.

Before leaving the job site, I made a list of the rail sections I would be replacing, their lengths and the number of posts I would need. Later that afternoon I found the house with the railing my customer liked, strolled up the walk, and began jotting down measurements. The family dog objected strenuously to my presence, but no one called the police.

Back at the shop I drew a full-scale section of the railing and a partial elevation showing the repeating elements. The next bit of work was to make layout sticks (or rods) showing the baluster spacing for the different rail sections. This would tell me the exact number of partial-and full-length balusters that I would need.

The Right Wood

I'm fortunate to have a good supplier who specializes in boat lumber. He carries premium grades of redwood, cedar, cypress, and Honduras mahogany, all of which resist decay well. I used cypress for the rails and balusters because it's less expensive and because the rough stock is a little thicker than the others. Cypress is mostly flatsawn from small trees, though, and the grain tends to lift if the wood isn't painted immediately.

Much of the western red cedar at this yard is vertical grain—the annual rings run perpendicular to the face—and hence inherently stable. I typically use it for wider pieces where cupping could be a problem. Square caps on posts fit this description because they are so short in length. They should always be made from vertical-grain material or they'll curl in the sun like potato chips.

For this job I bought 2-in.-thick cypress for the rails and balusters, 5/4 red cedar for the rail caps and post caps, and 1-in. cedar boards for the box newel posts.

When fungi sprout from railings, it's a rotten sign. Here is a close-up of the railing the author was hired to replace.

Bevels and Birds' Mouths

After cutting the lumber into rough lengths with a circular saw, I jointed, ripped, and thickness-planed the pieces to finish dimensions. Using a table saw, I beveled the top, middle, and bottom rail caps at 15°. Besides looking nice, the bevels keep water from sitting on what would otherwise be level surfaces.

Of all the woodwork exposed to the elements, none is so vulnerable as the white pine porch railing.

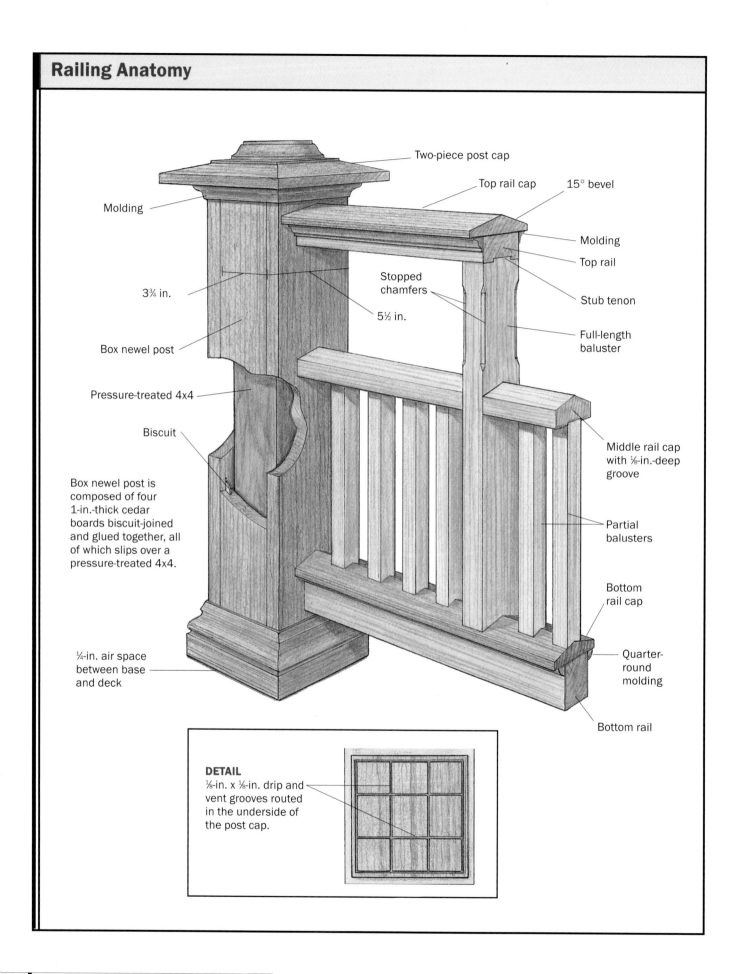

Two-piece post cap

Top rail cap

15° bevel

Molding

Molding

Top rail

3¾ in.

Stopped chamfers

Stub tenon

5½ in.

Full-length baluster

Box newel post

Pressure-treated 4x4

Biscuit

Middle rail cap with ⅛-in.-deep groove

Box newel post is composed of four 1-in.-thick cedar boards biscuit-joined and glued together, all of which slips over a pressure-treated 4x4.

Partial balusters

Bottom rail cap

Quarter-round molding

¼-in. air space between base and deck

Bottom rail

DETAIL
⅛-in. x ⅛-in. drip and vent grooves routed in the underside of the post cap.

I had to cut a bird's mouth on the bottom of each baluster so that the baluster would fit over the beveled cap on the bottom rail. I devised a shortcut to making these, as explained in the sidebar. I also cut birds' mouths in the full-length balusters with the same setup, but cut them one at a time because they were wider. These uprights also have decorative stopped chamfers routed into them. The chamfers bounce light smack into your eye in a most appealing way.

Next I set up the dado cutterhead on my table saw. I plowed a shallow groove for the partial balusters in the underside of the middle rail and another to receive the full-length balusters in the underside of the top rail. Although these grooves are a mere ⅛ in. deep, they made assembling the railing much easier and ensured positive alignment of the vertical members. The tops of the partial balusters are housed completely in the groove, but the tops of the full-length balusters also have stub tenons, cut on the radial-arm saw.

Box Newel Posts

Each box newel post is a two-part affair. I cut rough posts from pressure-treated 4x4 yellow pine and outfitted them with soldered copper base flashing (drawing, p.108). This flashing would later be heat-welded to the new roof surface (more on that in a minute). A finished cedar box newel post would slip over the rough post and receive the railings.

Because the sides of the box newels were to be butt-joined, two sides were left their full 5½-in. width, and the other two were ripped down to 3¾ in. so that the finished post would be square in cross section. I saved the rippings to make the quarter-round molding that's under the bottom rail cap.

The box newels were glued up with a generous helping of resorcinol to keep out

Shortcut for Cutting Birds' Mouths

Rather than make each bird's mouth individually for the balusters, I first crosscut my 2x6 baluster stock to finished length and joined one edge. I then ripped just enough off the opposite edge to make it parallel to the jointed edge. With the blade on my radial-arm saw raised off the table and tilted 15°, I made an angled crosscut halfway through the thickness of the baluster stock. Flipping the piece, I made the same cut from the opposite face. Individual balusters were then ripped from the 2x6, with each bird's mouth already formed.

moisture. Glue also does a better job of keeping the corner joints from opening up than nails do. To align the sides of the box newels during glue-up, I used three biscuit joints along the length of each side.

The last parts to be fabricated were the post caps. The square lower part of the cap is a shallow truncated pyramid, produced by making four consecutive bevel cuts on a table saw. I made the round upper part on a shaper. The two parts were glued together with the grain of each parallel to the other, so they would expand and contract in unison.

To reduce the amount of water running down the face of the post, I cut a drip groove around the underside of the cap with a ⅛-in. veiner bit mounted in a router table. Using the same bit, I also routed a series of ventilation grooves into the underside of the cap in a tic-tac-toe pattern (detail drawing, facing page). They allow air taken in at the bottom between the rough post and the box newels to escape at the top without letting in rain.

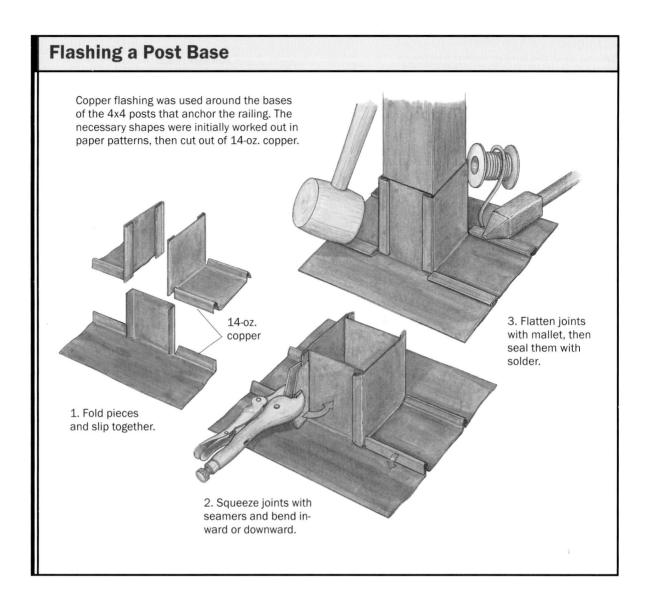

Copper flashing was used around the bases of the 4x4 posts that anchor the railing. The necessary shapes were initially worked out in paper patterns, then cut out of 14-oz. copper.

14-oz. copper

1. Fold pieces and slip together.

2. Squeeze joints with seamers and bend inward or downward.

3. Flatten joints with mallet, then seal them with solder.

Assembling the Rail Sections

I assembled the rail sections in the shop where I could count on dry weather and warm temperatures. The first step was to face-nail the bottom rail cap to the bottom rail. I placed the nails so that they would be covered subsequently by the ends of the balusters.

I toenailed the balusters in place with 4d galvanized finish nails. This was easy to do because the bevel and bird's-mouth joinery prevented the balusters from skidding around as I drove the nails.

The middle rail was cut into segments to fit between the full-length balusters. I took the lengths of the segments, along with the spacing for the partial balusters, directly from the layout on the bottom rail cap. Every other segment of the middle rail could be attached with 3-in. galvanized screws through the uprights. The intervening segments were toenailed with 8d galvanized finish nails. Then I face-nailed through the middle rail down onto the tops of the partial balusters. The top rail was screwed down onto the full-length balusters. I left the top-rail cap loose so that it could be trimmed on site for a tight fit between the newels.

Still in the shop, I caulked all the components with a paintable silicone caulk, primed the wood, and then painted it with a good-quality latex house paint. With a truckload of completed rail sections and posts I headed for the job site with my crew.

Installation

My roofing contractor had replaced the existing 90-lb. rolled roof over the garage with a single-ply modified-bitumen roof. One advantage of modified bitumen is that repairs and alterations can be heat-welded into the membrane long after the initial installation. This meant I didn't have to coordinate my schedule with that of the roofer to fuse the copper base flashings to the new roof. Flashing strips of the bitumen were melted on top of the copper flange, providing two layers of protection (including the copper) around the base of the post and a "through-flashed" layer of roofing beneath the post.

The railing is U-shaped in plan, and I anchored the two ends into the house. However, I didn't want to penetrate the roof membrane with framing or fasteners, so the newel posts are attached to the deck only by way of their flashings. Although this method of attaching the posts provides superb weather protection, the intermediate posts are a bit wobbly. This was okay for this particular deck because the railing is strictly decorative. Where a roof deck is subject to heavy use, the posts should be securely anchored to the framing.

With the rough posts in place, installation of the railing was straightforward. Box newels were slipped over the 4x4s and roughly plumbed. We stretched a line between corner newels and shimmed the intermediate newels up to the line. All box newels were held up off the deck at least ¼ in. to allow ventilation. The difference between the rough post dimenion (3½ in. by 3½ in.) and the internal dimension of the box newels (3¾ in. by 3¾ in.) allowed for

One of the advantages of a single-ply modified-bitumen roof is that repairs and alterations can be heat-welded to the membrane long after the initial installation. Here, flashing strips of bitumen, which cover the copper base flashings around the 4x4 posts, are being fused to the roof membrane.

some adjustment. When the newels were just where we wanted them, we simply nailed through the shims and into the rough posts.

In some cases rail sections had to be trimmed. When the fit was good, top, middle, and bottom rails were snugged up to the posts with galvanized screws. All that remained was to glue cypress plugs into the counterbored holes and shave them flush.

Scott McBride is a contributing editor of Fine Homebuilding *magazine and the author of* Build Like a Pro™: Windows and Doors, *published by The Taunton Press.*

Where a roof deck is subject to heavy use, the posts should be securely anchored to the framing.

Exterior-Trim Details That Last

■ BY JOHN MICHAEL DAVIS

Drainage mat gives moisture a way out. Because even the best caulk joint can fail, a ⅜-in.-thick drainage mat is applied between this porch post and its base trim. Any moisture that gets past the caulk is able to run out beneath the front baseboard, which is left uncaulked.

The old saying "It's better to be lucky than smart" certainly applies to New Orleans, Louisiana. Considering the rot-acceleration chamber that passes for a climate here, it's remarkable that New Orleans has more nineteenth-century houses than any other city in the country. Although it's tempting to credit the skill of old-time carpenters who built things to last, the only reason all these houses are still standing is luck. When the first Europeans arrived, almost every acre of land in New Orleans was concealed beneath a massive canopy of old-growth cypress trees. Clearing the land for development released a seemingly unlimited supply of one of the heartiest building materials on the planet.

The old-timers didn't worry about back-priming, drainage planes, or caulking. They just nailed together two pieces of wood and walked away; no fungus was going to take a bite out of a 2,000-year-old chunk of cypress. Do that with the fast-growth sapwood we have to work with today, and you can be sure the forces of decay will start moving in before the extension cords are rolled up.

Caulk Is the First Line of Defense

Among all the places where rot can secure a foothold in exterior woodwork, caulked joints are probably the most vulnerable. Seasonal changes in temperature and humidity cause wooden trim elements to expand and contract. Unless caulk has the flexibility to accommodate this movement, sooner or later, the bead will crack, and water will seep in. From that point on, the caulk actually does more harm than good because it allows water to soak into the wood while it restricts air circulation that would promote drying.

My approach to protecting vulnerable exterior trim is twofold: First, I try to create a caulk joint that can weather many seasons of expansion and contraction. I've been around long enough to know that even the best caulk joint will eventually fail, however, so as often as possible, I also build a path for moisture to escape when that happens.

Backer Rod Gives Caulk the Freedom to Move

There are two ways to create a caulk joint that can handle expansion and contraction: Either reduce the amount of movement or increase the ability of caulk to move. I do both. Certain species of wood, such as pressure-treated southern yellow pine, are inherently unstable, so I try not to use them when given a choice. For exterior trim, I prefer to use the highest-quality kiln-dried lumber I can find; in my area, that's either mahogany, Spanish cedar, or all-heart redwood. I also fully prime every piece of trim, and I assemble permanent (crackproof) miter joints using biscuits and marine epoxy.

I increase the ability of the caulk to move with the wood by applying high-quality polyurethane caulk (sidebar p. 117) on top of a backer rod to create a two-sided caulk joint. (Caulk doesn't adhere to the foam backer rod.) The biggest mistake most amateur

caulkers make is to fill the joint completely where two pieces of wood meet. This procedure not only wastes caulk but also creates a three-sided joint that's prone to failure: The caulk adhering to the bottom and to both sides of the joint is left little room for movement. A two-sided joint—one in which the caulk bonds to the sides but not the bottom of the joint—allows the caulk to expand and contract like an accordion.

In principle, creating a two-sided caulk joint is simple enough: Just cover the bottom of the joint with a bond breaker, any material that will prevent the caulk from bonding. If a joint is shallow and cannot be enlarged, special Fine Line tapes are used as bond breakers, but these tapes can be difficult to work with. An easier, better approach is to enlarge the joint to make space for a foam backer rod.

Caulk Needs Help to Stay Flexible

Backer board

Caulk

Trim board

Caulk that is allowed to bond to all sides of a joint cannot expand and contract without becoming unstuck.

A foam backer rod helps caulk behave like an accordion in response to seasonal expansion and contraction.

Backer board

Caulk

⅜-in. backer rod

Trim board

Even the best caulk joint will eventually fail, so as often as possible, I build a path for moisture to escape when that happens.

Active Drainage Planes Protect Vulnerable Trim

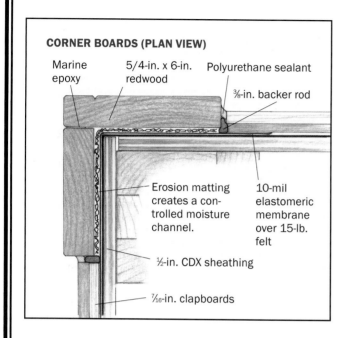

CORNER BOARDS (PLAN VIEW)

Marine epoxy

5/4-in. x 6-in. redwood

Polyurethane sealant

⅜-in. backer rod

Erosion matting creates a controlled moisture channel.

10-mil elastomeric membrane over 15-lb. felt

½-in. CDX sheathing

⁷⁄₁₆-in. clapboards

PORCH SKIRTING (ELEVATION)

5/4 porch flooring

Polyurethane sealant

Erosion matting creates a ³⁄₁₆-in. (nominal) gap.

1x8 red-cypress skirtboard

8d galvanized finish nails

Router-cut profile

2x10 pressure-treated band joist

2x10 pressure-treated floor joist

Here are just three examples of how well-planned caulk details used in combination with an active drainage channel offer two layers of protection to the most-exposed parts of a house.

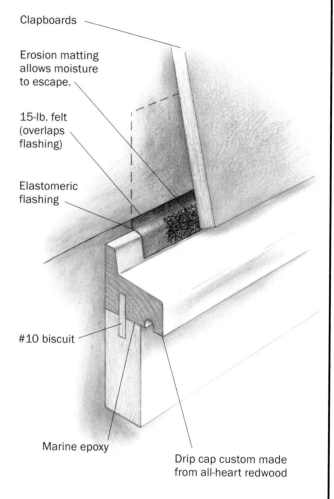

WATER TABLE AND DRIP CAPS

Clapboards

Erosion matting allows moisture to escape.

15-lb. felt (overlaps flashing)

Elastomeric flashing

#10 biscuit

Marine epoxy

Drip cap custom made from all-heart redwood

Wherever there's a place that two pieces of exterior trim must fit together tightly, my standard procedure is to cut a ³⁄₁₆-in.-wide by ½-in.-deep rabbet into the inside edges of the trim pieces (drawing, p. 111). After the trim is assembled, I compress a ⅜-in. dia. poly foam backer rod into the bottom of the joint. This ⅜-in. backer rod leaves enough space on top for a ³⁄₁₆-in. wide by ⅛-in. deep bead of caulk.

Erosion Mat Gives Moisture an Out

Unfortunately, the best caulking job doesn't come with a lifetime guarantee. No matter how conscientious I am, at some point in time, somewhere along the joint, I know the caulk is going to fail. Failure could be caused by a minor installation flaw such as a drop of sweat on the wood or an undetected bubble in the bead. If I'm lucky, the joint will last the life of the sealant (20 years tops). But at that point, no one else is going to lavish the same attention on the work as I did. So to ensure long-term survival of exterior trim that depends on caulk for survival, I build in a means for moisture to escape.

An escape route for moisture could be something as simple as a couple of circular louvers near the top and bottom of a hollow column to promote air circulation. On the other hand, a fully exposed trim element such as a corner board, drip cap, or porch skirting (drawing, facing page) that has nothing but caulk to protect its innards from wind-driven rain or splash-back requires an active drainage plane.

Not long ago, I had to repair built-up posts that supported a railing on an uncovered second-story porch. In this case, most of the rot damage occurred when water seepage became trapped between the applied baseboards and the bottom of the post carcase. To prevent the same type of damage from happening in the future, I created a simple drainage plane to give moisture a way out (drawing, right).

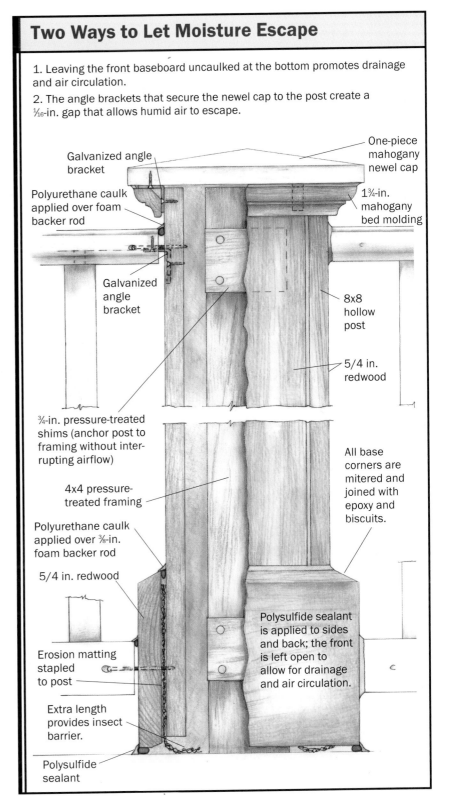

Two Ways to Let Moisture Escape

1. Leaving the front baseboard uncaulked at the bottom promotes drainage and air circulation.
2. The angle brackets that secure the newel cap to the post create a ¹⁄₁₆-in. gap that allows humid air to escape.

Galvanized angle bracket

One-piece mahogany newel cap

Polyurethane caulk applied over foam backer rod

1¾-in. mahogany bed molding

Galvanized angle bracket

8x8 hollow post

5/4 in. redwood

¾-in. pressure-treated shims (anchor post to framing without interrupting airflow)

4x4 pressure-treated framing

All base corners are mitered and joined with epoxy and biscuits.

Polyurethane caulk applied over ⅜-in. foam backer rod

5/4 in. redwood

Polysulfide sealant is applied to sides and back; the front is left open to allow for drainage and air circulation.

Erosion matting stapled to post

Extra length provides insect barrier.

Polysulfide sealant

Any type of rot-resistant shim stock can be used to create a drainage plane, but the best material I've found is Enkamat® #7010, a ¼-in.-thick mat of entangled nylon filaments that is manufactured for use as an

Creating the Perfect Caulk Joint

Before I apply any caulk, I make sure all the wood surfaces are fully primed; if some of the woodwork in the photos looks unprimed, it's because my favorite primer (Primkote #8006-1) is a two-part epoxy that goes on clear. Wherever I've installed backer rod, I use my finger as a gauge to make sure the rods are deep enough to allow a minimum sealant depth of ⅛ in.

A professional-grade caulking gun is a must for applying the thick polyurethane sealants (photo 4); I've never given much thought to whether it's better to push or pull the gun while applying the caulk, however; because to me the gun is simply a delivery device. I tool every bead of sealant I apply, and my favorite tools are my thumb and forefinger. (They're just always there; what can I say?)

Polyurethane has to be cleaned up with mineral spirits, and over the years, I've developed chemical sensitivity to prolonged exposure, so I wear 4-mil disposable nitrile gloves almost all the time. It's not always easy to get crisp drags with gloves on, so when the appearance of the joint is crucial, I will use a bare finger if nothing else works, but I prefer to use a tool.

I think I've tried every tool specifically designed for dragging caulk, and I've never had much luck with any of them. What works best for me is a 3-in. artist's palette knife (photo 1). Looking like a miniature bricklayer's trowel, a palette knife has a long, thin, tapered blade with a rounded tip that's flexible enough to offer precise control. The blade is also polished and slick enough to get a really smooth drag, especially if it's regularly wiped off and lubricated with solvent.

1. Palette knife tools visible joints.

2. Mineral spirits remove excess caulk.

3. Backer rod allows caulk to flex.

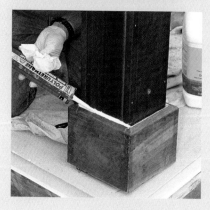

4. Polyurethane is the first line of defense.

Modern Materials Protect Historic Trim

Moisture that seeped in through failed caulk joints caused extensive rot damage to this 100-year-old column base. After the damaged areas were rebuilt with epoxy, air vents were added, and a variety of modern tools and materials was used to retrofit working caulk joints.

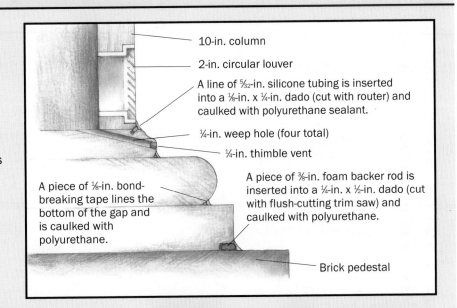

10-in. column

2-in. circular louver

A line of 5/32-in. silicone tubing is inserted into a 1/8-in. x 1/4-in. dado (cut with router) and caulked with polyurethane sealant.

1/4-in. weep hole (four total)

1/4-in. thimble vent

A piece of 1/8-in. bond-breaking tape lines the bottom of the gap and is caulked with polyurethane.

A piece of 3/8-in. foam backer rod is inserted into a 1/4-in. x 1/2-in. dado (cut with flush-cutting trim saw) and caulked with polyurethane.

Brick pedestal

A corner-grooving tool carves a 1/8-in. dado into the joint where the column shaft meets the upper torus of the base.

Custom-mounted on a Plexiglas® base, a flush-cutting saw cuts a rabbet where the edge of the plinth meets the brick pier.

When standard backer rods are too thick, other materials are pressed into service. Some 5/32-in. silicone weatherstripping fits the 1/8-in. groove at the top of the base.

Fine Line tape backs up the caulk joint between the upper and lower torus sections.

erosion matting (sidebar, p. 116). After cutting the mat to size with a utility knife, I wrapped it tightly around the post and then fastened it with staples.

To allow for the mat's thickness, I added 3/8 in. to the length of each baseboard. After cutting all the baseboards to length, I pre-assembled three sides of the box before slipping it around the post. While applying slight pressure on the corners to compress the mat, I checked the reveals by sight before I tacked the baseboards using an air nailer (photo, p. 110).

After the final side of the baseboard was glued and tacked in place, I filled the gap around the top with 3/8-in. backer rod. The

The Right Stuff May Be Hard to Find

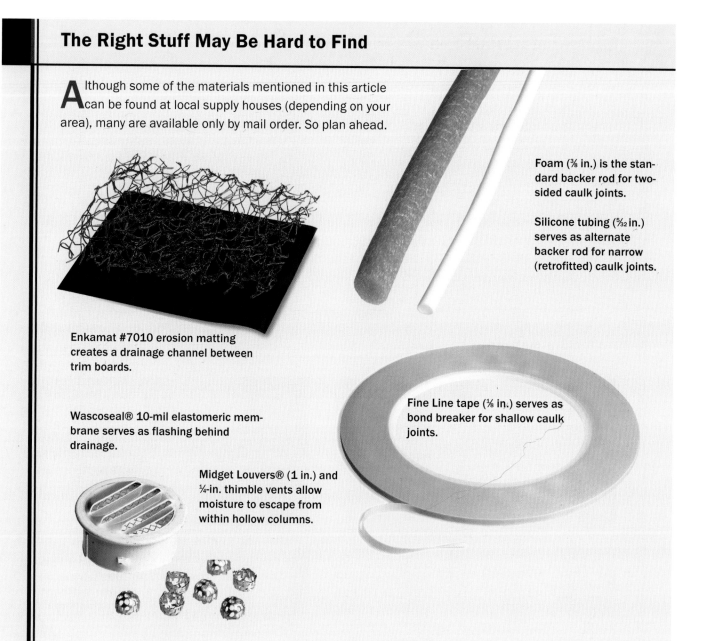

Although some of the materials mentioned in this article can be found at local supply houses (depending on your area), many are available only by mail order. So plan ahead.

Foam (⅜ in.) is the standard backer rod for two-sided caulk joints.

Silicone tubing (⁵⁄₃₂ in.) serves as alternate backer rod for narrow (retrofitted) caulk joints.

Enkamat #7010 erosion matting creates a drainage channel between trim boards.

Fine Line tape (⅛ in.) serves as bond breaker for shallow caulk joints.

Wascoseal® 10-mil elastomeric membrane serves as flashing behind drainage.

Midget Louvers® (1 in.) and ¼-in. thimble vents allow moisture to escape from within hollow columns.

best tool I've found for forcing backer rod into a tight gap is a window-screen spline roller (photo 3, p.114). Because this tool has different-size wheels on each end, I choose the end that fits the situation best and simply roll the rope in with one hand while stretching it slightly with my other hand. Using a finger as a gauge, I roll back and forth over the backer rod until the top is at least ⅛ in. below the top of the baseboard. Then I cover the backer rod with a ³⁄₁₆-in. bead of polyurethane caulk (photo 4, p.114).

Hardware Creates Breathing Room

Other weak points on the built-up post are the post-cap assembly and the joint where the railings meet the post. If the railing is thick enough, I'll make space for ⅜-in. backer rod by rabbeting the edge the same way I described earlier. If I'm installing a narrow railing, like the one on this job, however, I cut the railing ¼ in. short and mount it on top of a galvanized angle bracket (drawing, p.113).

The Best Caulks Are Flexible and Paintable SB4

Polyurethane sealant is my preferred exterior caulk. Although more than twice as expensive as premium acrylic latex, polyurethane's vastly superior adhesion and flexibility make it a bargain. I use Sikaflex 1a, a European polyurethane available only through marine suppliers or by mail order. Recently, my local suppliers have begun stocking polyurethane sealants from Macklanburg-Duncan. One day, I'll give them a try.

Although polyurethane is my standard exterior caulk, for super-critical joints—such as the front edge of a threshold—I use polysulfide. Polysulfide costs three times as much as Sikaflex and takes three days to seven days to dry. Nevertheless, polysulfide retains significantly more flexibility far longer than polyurethane and is sandable. Where appearance is critical, sandability allows me to create seamless fillets. I use 3M #101 polysulfide , but have only small (3-oz.) tubes on hand because they don't keep well after opening.

Silicone is highly flexible and adhesive, but I don't use it often because—despite some marketing claims—it can't be painted. Where wood has been painted or where trim elements are metal, glass, or masonry, silicone is a more effective caulk than

3M® #101 polysulfide

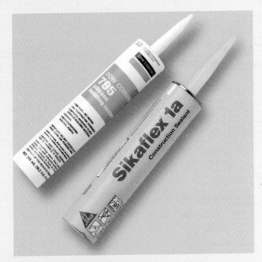

Dow Corning® #795 silicone sealant and Sikaflex®, a polyurethane sealant

polyurethane. All silicones are not alike, however; in my opinion, Dow Corning #795 is thicker, more adhesive, and more toolable than anything I can get at a hardware store, and it costs only a dollar or two more a tube.

Those handy angle brackets also make it easy to create a breathing space while mounting the post cap. Using a scrap of cardboard as a temporary shim between the top of the post and the cap, I installed two 1-in. angle brackets on each side to anchor the post to the cap; then I removed the shim and covered the brackets with a bed molding. I caulked the joint where the molding met the cap but left the bottom of the molding uncaulked to promote air circulation.

Older Trim Needs Help, Too

Although modern lumber is more susceptible to rot, even old-growth cypress can deteriorate after years of neglect. When I have to repair localized rot damage on significant structures such as windowsills or porch columns, I try to rebuild the missing or damaged sections in place using epoxy. Wherever a failed caulk joint was the source of moisture, I retrofit the structure with working caulk joints. I also try to install air vents and weep holes that could help to promote drying (drawing, p. 115).

Recently, I used these strategies to create working caulk joints on the base of a 10-in. round column. As with most cases, the worst rot damage occurred at the top and the bottom of the base. At these places, I used a couple of specialty tools (not made for the purpose) to carve out the space for backer rods.

At the top of the base, where the column shaft rested on the upper torus ring of the base, I was able to use a corner-grooving tool, which is intended for installing weather stripping in old door frames, to carve a ⅛-in.-wide by ¼-in.-deep dado (top left photo, p. 115). I've also been able to make this cut, although not as easily, using a cordless drill equipped with a ⅛-in. ball-shaped die-grinder bit. The only problem with carving a narrow groove such as this one is that stan-

dard backer rods are too wide; fortunately, I have found an alternative, which I'll describe in a moment.

Before completing the caulking detail on the top of the column base, I used the flush-cutting saw I'd normally use for trimming door jambs to make a space for standard backer rod underneath the base (top right photo, p. 115). The flush-cutting saw allowed me to place a ½-in.-deep saw kerf, ¼ in. up from the bottom. I needed a few swipes with a sharp chisel to remove the waste, and the base was ready for backer rod.

After blowing out the sawdust, I coated both grooves with Primkote #8006-1, a fast-drying epoxy primer that did not clog the groove as most primers would have. Five minutes later, when the primer was dry, I inserted a ⅜-in. foam backer rod in the groove beneath the base. In the narrow groove on top, I inserted my stand-in for backer rod, a length of ⁵⁄₃₂-in. silicone tubing (bottom left-photo, p. 115) that, like the cutting tool, was also intended for weatherstripping (sidebar, p. 116).

Although the top and bottom of this column suffered the most rot damage, I also caulked the two middle joints where the individual torus sections came together. Both joints had enough cleavage between them for caulk but not backer rod, so I used bond-breaking tape instead (bottom right photo, p. 115). To prevent a three-sided bond that would crack and fail, I lined the bottom of each joint with ⅛-in.-wide (#218) Fine Line tape. Once all the bond breakers were in place, I caulked all the joints with polyurethane sealant and tooled them smooth, confident that this column will be around a lot longer than I will.

John Michael Davis is a restoration carpenter in New Orleans, Louisiana.

Sources

Abatron
5501 95th Ave.
Kenosha, WI 53144
(800) 445-1754
PrimKote #8006-1

Charette
31 Olympia Ave.
Box 4010
Woburn, MA 01888
(800) 367-3729
Palette knife

Colbond Geosynthetics
P.O. Box 1057
Enka, NC 28728
(800) 365-7391
Enkamat #7010

Crain Power Tools
156 S. Milpitas Blvd.
Milpitas, CA 95035
(408) 946-6100
Flush cutting saw

Gougeon Bros. Inc.
100 Patterson Ave.
Bay City, MI 48707
(989) 684-7286
Marine epoxy

Midget Louver Co.
671 Naugatuck Ave.
Milford, CT 06460
(800) 643-4381
Midget Louvers and thimble vents

Resource Conservation Technology Inc.;
2633 N. Calvert St.
Baltimore, MD 21218
(410) 366-1146
Sikaflex 1a, corner grooving tool

York Manufacturing Inc.
43 Community Dr.
Sanford, ME 04073
(800) 551-2828
Wascoseal

Learning Curves for Decks

■ BY SCOTT PADGETT

lumb, level, and square. For me, these three building commandments always included an implied fourth: straight. But after 20 years, I found working to these rules less and less of a challenge. Then I discovered curves. Not only do I think them more graceful and pleasing to the eye but I also have encountered a whole new set of challenges. I've since built more than a dozen curved decks for clients, plus one for myself. Surprisingly, I've learned that curved work looks harder than it really is.

Standard Framing and a 1x4 Trammel

Framing the undercarriage of a curved deck is relatively straightforward. One difference is that you often can't use a single straight girder to support the cantilevered joists of a curved deck. If you did, the joists in the center of the curve would end up cantilevering too far. The solution is to use two or more girders configured in a wide V to support the curves (top photos, p. 120).

Conventional Framing Supports Curved Decks

Although curved decks look difficult, the framing is simple enough. The key difference is in arranging the girders to avoid overcantilevering the joists. This is usually done by setting several girders at angles rather than the typical single girder that supports most decks.

Angled girders avoid excessively cantilevered joists. Joist length varies on curved decks, so the author runs them long and cuts them to length in place.

Locating the Centerpoint

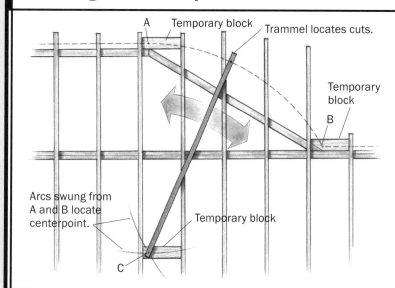

A — Temporary block

Trammel locates cuts.

Temporary block

B

Arcs swung from A and B locate centerpoint.

Temporary block

C

If you know the radius and the location of the intersection of the curved and straight sections of the deck (points A and B), finding the centerpoint (C) is simple. Drawn using temporary blocks and the same trammel, arcs swung from A and B intersect at C, the centerpoint. Reversing the trammel marks the radius on the joists.

A trammel made from a 1x4 lays out big radii. A pencil placed in a drilled hole marks the radius atop the joists. The trammel pivots on a nail that has been driven in a temporary block (drawing).

Lines squared down from the trammel marks guide the saw in cutting the joists to length. The bevel of the saw is adjusted for each cut.

Blocking nailed between the joists keeps the ends from flexing as the laminations are bent around them, provides backing for stapling the laminations, and makes a solid attachment point for newels.

I allow all joists to run long, then cut them to length after marking the correct radius. Working from an accurate scale drawing of the framing greatly simplifies this process because it allows me to select and install joists of the proper length.

After the girders and joists are in place, a trammel consisting of a 1x4 with a nail in one end and a pencil in a hole drilled through the other end is all it takes to lay out the perimeter radius (bottom left photo, facing page). I nail a 2x6 block between joists to provide a pivot point for the trammel (drawing, facing page). The radius is marked on each joist's top edge, and a cutline is squared down its face. The angle of cut will be different for each joist and is easily determined by lining up the blade on the radius mark, and then locking in the angle on the saw (bottom center photo, facing page). When all joists have been trimmed, I install blocking between their ends to provide solid bearing for the railing posts (bottom right photo, facing page).

Rip Good Wood into Narrow Strips for Bending

I use air-dried redwood for curved elements. Kiln drying makes wood more brittle and less resilient, so I don't recommend using kiln-dried wood for curves. Unless I'm steam-bending, when the initial moisture content of the wood makes little difference, I avoid green lumber because of the shrinkage potential. For this deck, I used air-dried 2x6 B-grade redwood as deck boards. I picked out the best boards to rip into strips to be laminated into curved rails and fascias. I chose only wood with growth rings that were ⅛ in. or less apart. Wood with more widely spaced growth rings can split apart at the rings while it's being bent.

The tighter the radii are, the thinner the laminations should be. For a 5-ft. radius, I use ⅛-in.-thick stock; ¼-in.-thick material bends to a 6-ft. radius, ⅜-in. material con-

forms to a 10-ft. radius, ½-in bends to a 16-ft. radius, and ¾-in.-thick material takes care of everything larger than a 20-ft. radius. For radii less than 5 ft., I steam the wood to make it pliable enough to bend (sidebar pp. 124-125). For decks with multiple radii, I find it more efficient to cut all the wood to the proper thickness to form the tightest curve. This practice also eliminates the possibility of mixing materials of differing thicknesses.

Also, a 3-in.-wide piece of stock of any thickness is more flexible than a 6-in.-wide strip of the same thickness (and is easier to rip on a table saw). The formula above is for 3½-in. or narrower pieces. When I need to make up a wider lamination, I lay the strips together into the lamination (photo, right). For example, all the fascia on this deck are 1½ in. thick and 5½ in. wide. Instead of trying to work with 5½-in.-thick stock, I ripped 2x6s in half; then from the resulting 2x3s, I ripped the twelve ¼-in. thick strips that formed the laminations.

Defects can cause the wood to fracture, so I inspect it carefully for checks, knots, and other problems before ripping it into strips.

TIP

Defects can cause the wood to fracture, so inspect it carefully for checks, knots, and other problems before ripping it into strips.

To make up the 5½-in. wide fascia, the author glued layers of 2¾-in. wide strips side by side. After ripping a 2x6, he resawed the 2¾-in. wide halves into thin, bendable strips using a 10-in. table saw. Waterproof glue and staples make quick, reliable laminations. The glue is applied with a disposable paint roller to ensure uniform coverage (photo, left). A helper positioning the strips eases stapling them in the correct location (photo, above).

The Joists Are the Bending Form

To make the fascia, I stapled the first strip to the joist ends with 1½-in. long, ¼-in. crown galvanized staples. I spread TiteBond® II, a waterproof glue, on the face of the second strip and stapled it below the first. I was careful to keep this strip as flush as possible with the first. Then I spread glue on the strips for the second layer in the laminations (bottom photo, p. 121).

Each layer was stapled to the previous layer with the staples spaced to close any voids. Because of the blocking between the joist ends, I didn't have to worry about staples sticking dangerously out of the back of the fascia. I putty the staple holes in the last layer with Color Putty® after finishing the deck.

With six layers in place, I gave the glue a day to dry. Then I belt-sanded the joint in the fascia's center, where the 2¾-in. strips meet.

Bending Forms for the Railing

The next step was to locate newel posts along the curves. I laid out the locations of these posts by measuring the length of the arc with a tape and dividing this number into equal spaces. Because tight-radius laminations exert more pressure on the posts (which serve as forms for all but the tightest radii), posts on a large radius can be set far-

Jig Marks the Radius on the Decking

After trimming most of the scrap from the decking, the author marks the final curve with this jig (photo). Two points of its bottom slide along the fascia, and the pencil marks the cut (drawing). This method ensures that the decking follows the fascia.

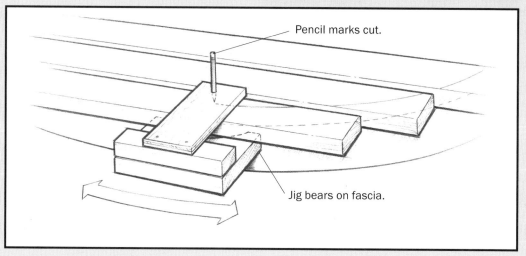

Pencil marks cut.

Jig bears on fascia.

ther apart than posts on a tight curve. On my deck, I set the posts on about 4-ft. centers for the 10-ft. radius section and on slightly less than 3-ft. centers for the 6-ft. radius section.

A word of caution: Bending wood can snap it. I work from the inside of the curve so that I'm not in the line of fire if a lamination breaks.

I marked each post in place by holding it tangent to the inside edge of the curved fascia and scribing its bottom to the joist blocking. Then I notched the posts using a bandsaw. When all posts were set, I cut an additional 2x6 block to fit between the joists and against the inside edge of each post to provide support on three sides of each post (photo above). The posts were further secured with ½-in. galvanized machine bolts.

Before I could bend the railings, I had to lay the deck boards. Curves affect deckboard layout in several ways. Because the newel posts are tangent to the curve, abutting deck boards require notching at different angles. Occasionally, a post falling in the center of a deck board demands a pocket cut. I lay out such cuts using a scrap of post and set the angle with a sliding bevel. Once the cuts are marked, I drill a hole large enough for a jigsaw blade and cut the post's hole, back-cutting slightly to ease slipping the board over the post.

I rough-cut deck boards about 3 in. past the fascia. To mark the finish cut, I made a jig out of scrap 2x6, which bears on the curved fascia below (sidebar, facing page). A pencil atop the jig marked an even overhang. A jigsaw with a sharp blade made the final cut, and I belt-sanded the edge smooth and fair. When screwing down decking near the curved fascia, I drove the screws into the blocking so that I wouldn't wedge apart the layers in the lamination.

Blocking braces the newels. Because the newels are the forms for the railing, they must be braced to stay plumb while the railing is being bent. Bolts will reinforce this connection.

Horizontal Rails Preserve the View

I designed my rails to be horizontal because they emphasize the deck's contours. Be careful with this design if you have children who might climb the rail or if you live in an area where horizontal rails are code restricted.

Bending the railings was similar to bending the fascia. The main difference was that the rails were narrow enough (3½ in. at most) that I could make them from one width of stock. Also, except for the top laminated rail, each lamination consisted of six ¼-in. layers for both visual and physical strength. The rails were bent in place and stapled with ¼-in. crown galvanized staples sized to penetrate all layers but not protrude.

To support a narrow strip during glue up, an extra joist serves as a bench. This strip will be applied to the curved rail, partially completed in the background, then secured with staples while the glue sets.

Tight Curves Require Steam

The most demanding of all the curves on this deck occurred at the balcony, where the radii varied from 30 in. to as tight as 9 in. These tight curves required steam-bending. I use a low-tech device.

After finding that my Coleman® camp stove was inadequate, I used a 50,000-BTU propane burner for the heat source. A *new* 2½-gal. gasoline can is the steam generator.

A length of radiator hose sized to fit tightly into the spout of the gas can connects the can to the steam box, a 10-ft. length of 6-in. schedule-40 PVC pipe. Caps are glued on one end and left loose on the other. A hole drilled in the pipe's bottom accepts the radiator hose, and four other ½-in.-dia. holes let condensate drain and avoid pressure buildup.

A narrow section of aluminum grille, also from the hardware store, keeps the redwood off the bottom of the tube so that steam can circulate. The whole setup cost less than $100.

Plywood Forms Shape the Layers

For curves this tight, it's necessary to clamp the wood to forms. I made mine of ¾-in. plywood top and bottom, with 1½-in. blocks between. The forms were 3½ in. wide, the same thickness as the posts, which expedited the process by allowing the inside and outside pieces to be clamped simultaneously.

Because I used water-activated polyurethane glue for these rails and because I was going to steam the wood, I cut the railing strips from unseasoned redwood 4x4s. I made them all ¾6 in. thick and kept them stacked in the order in which they were cut to keep glue joints as inconspicuous as possible.

Before placing the strips in the steamer, I put ⅛-in.-thick wooden spacers between the layers to allow better circulation of the steam. Rubber bands hold the bundles of wood together to ease handling the material.

I fire up the burner and wait until steam begins pouring out of the holes in the bottom of the tube. Then I remove the loose cap, place the bundle of strips in the tube and replace the cap. I use gloves and turn my face away while placing and removing steamed pieces. After about 45 minutes, I remove the hot bundle, clamp the pieces around the form and let them cool for an hour or two.

When the redwood has cooled, I remove the clamps and start applying glue. For this project, plastic tape on the forms and wax paper beneath prevented gluing the forms, the redwood, and the workbench together. Clamps were placed about 3 in. apart, and each assembly was left to cure overnight.

Once the wood is removed from the form, installation is simply a matter of screwing the rail to the posts, and then building a cap rail, as I did for the larger-radius railing.

A *new* gas can—filled with water—is the heart of the steam generator. A propane burner provides the heat, and a radiator hose brings the steam to the PVC-pipe steam chamber. Holes in the PVC drain condensate and prevent pressure buildup.

Steamed-redwood strips easily bend to tight radii. The author clamps the steamed strips to plywood forms for several hours until the wood cools. Then he unclamps the strips, spreads glue, and reclamps them.

A pencil scribes the curve on the segmented 2x8 cap rail. Intermediate 4x4 blocks (foreground) support joints in the cap rail that don't fall on newels as well as provide blocking for the top bent rails.

At the top rail, I divided the six layers so that three layers went on each side of the posts to support both edges of the cap rail. The cap rail was cut from segments of 2x8 redwood, mitered to place the splices over posts or over 4x4 blocks placed between the top rails (photo, above). In this case, I used kiln-dried wood to minimize shrinkage and to keep the miters as tight as possible.

The larger the radius, the greater the length of each cap-rail segment that could be cut from a 2x8 and still leave a ½-in. overhang. For the 10-ft. radius, each segment was about 24 in. long, and the 6-ft. radius allowed only about 16-in. segments. When all the segments had been mitered and tacked in place, I scribed the curve on the underside of the blanks using a pencil that was taped to a shim and then held flat against the top rail. The cap-rail segments were then removed, and the curves were cut on a bandsaw. During the final installation, I cut a #20 biscuit into each of the miters and applied glue to mating surfaces.

A light pass with a belt sander removed the bandsaw marks and smoothed the curve. I screwed the cap rail into the posts and blocks only, not into the top rail, to avoid splits.

Scott Padgett is a carpenter and designer in Idyllwild, California.

A Comfortable Outdoor Bench

■ BY DAVID BRIGHT

A good carpenter always takes pride in a well-done job, but some projects are especially gratifying. Such was the reward that Mark Schouten and Doug TeVelde got from building a red-cedar bench on a deck overlooking the placid waters of Lake Whatcom near Bellingham, Washington. The bench was designed by David Hall.

The bench had to meet three criteria: It had to be truly comfortable; it had to survive in a damp, rainy climate; it had to complement its spectacular setting and yet blend with it.

Many wood benches are uncomfortable. They make you slouch forward, or they make you wish you could. Some benches cut

Comfort that stands up to the weather. By slanting or curving most of the surfaces on this bench, the builders were able to create a seat that is truly comfortable. The slopes and the curves also eliminate horizontal planes on which standing water can collect.

Built for Comfort

The seat supports dip in a curve ¾ in. from level. Each seat support is sandwiched between two 2x4 back supports that are canted 10° from plumb.

4x4 cap

Stainless-steel screws

¾-in. x 2¼-in. cap nailer

2x4 back supports canted 10° from plumb

1x4 back rail stands ¹⁄₁₆-in. proud of back supports.

15 in.

36 in.

16 in.

2x6 face piece

Seat support made of laminated 2x4s

Bottom back rail butts into seat supports.

4-in. stainless-steel screws

Back support notched around decking.

Galvanized carriage bolts

you behind the knees or across the back. But this bench is made for comfort. The back leans out 10° from vertical, and the seat dips in a curve about ¾ in. below horizontal—just enough to allow your back to rest naturally against the rails.

As well as making the bench comfortable, the slopes and the curves diminish the number of horizontal planes on the bench and allow few places for rainwater to collect. To further the bench's weather resistance, the wood was spaced to allow air to circulate, and all fasteners were galvanized or made of stainless steel.

Back and Seat Supports

Before assembling the bench, all the pieces of clear red cedar used in the construction were run through a surface sander. The extra effort spent dressing the wood in the beginning saved considerable time at the end when it was time to apply the finish to the bench.

The bench frame consists of seat supports and back supports. The back supports are made of 2x4s. Before attaching them to the deck, we dadoed the supports to accept the 1x4 back rails. The back supports are canted 10° from plumb and, as the drawing at left shows, we cut the bottom ends of the back supports to fit against the deck frame, where two galvanized carriage bolts and a little construction adhesive hold them solid and tight. Two back supports sandwich each seat support.

The seat supports are made of 2x4s laminated with exterior urethane resin glue. To attach the seat supports to the deck, we angled 4-in. stainless-steel screws through the decking from underneath. Throughout the assembly process we tried to fasten either from underneath or on a vertical surface; our idea was to avoid areas where water could penetrate the wood through the holes made by the screws. We also wanted to avoid showing any fasteners.

We ran a horizontal 2x6 face piece around the inside perimeter of the seat. The face piece is flush with the top edge of the seat support and was beveled (on a table saw) to continue the curving top plane of the seat support. The face piece helps finish the design of the bench; it also supports the first row of 2x4s that make the seat.

Curves, Cants, and Compound Miters

The first row of 2x4s that make the bench's seat extends over the face piece about ½ in. The 2x4s were installed beginning at the inside edge—the edge that your knees rest against. Working toward the back rest gave us room to fasten screws into the miter joint at the bench's two inside corners. If we had started from the outside and worked inward toward the front, the previous row of mitered 2x4s would not have allowed us to fasten the next row. A good adhesive caulking seals the end grain of the miter and helps keep the joint tight.

If the seat had no curve, mitering its joints would have been a matter of cutting good, familiar 45s. But the curve demanded a compound miter, and a different one for each row—a fact that will no doubt be lost on the folks who will sit there. On the inside row, the miter must be undercut; on the second, not so much; the third is almost perpendicular; and the last miter is shorter on the surface than on the bottom. The safest way to get the right compound cut was to use two scrap pieces of 2x4 to test the angles. You may draw like Frank Lloyd Wright and calculate like Einstein, but when it comes to making that critical cut, you'd better test first.

If you're off a bit, you can change the angle of your blade or remove some wood with a chisel or a block plane. Remember, red cedar is soft, and it's easy to overcorrect. (You know the story: Soon your board is too short, and your temper is shorter.)

The horizontal back rails are 1x4s, which were carefully let into the canted 2x4 back supports. The rails extend about ⅟₁₆-in. past the back supports. Because of the 10° angle of the back, the corner miters are compound angles, too. Construction adhesive and two nails from each direction hold the corners tight. To avoid splitting, we predrilled the corners before nailing. The mitered corners seem to hang in midair, but they are as strong as can be.

Before the rail cap was installed, a ¾-in. by 2¼-in. cedar strip running the length of the back rest was notched flush into the top of each 2x4 back support. This strip provided a way to screw from underneath into the 4x4 cedar cap. The corners of the cap were

The finished bench complements its spectacular setting.

also mitered at a compound angle very similar to the first miter of the seat.

After the cap was installed, we touched up the wood with 150-grit sandpaper. For comfort's sake, we made sure all the sharp edges of the bench were eased with sandpaper. Sanding also removes nicks and pencil lines that are unavoidable during construction. We didn't want these small imperfections to get sealed into the wood. After sanding, the bench was sealed with a semitransparent stain.

It's not often that people in our business get to build a project so perfectly suited to its location. We did our best, and the results rewarded us.

David Bright is a custom home builder in Lynden, Washington.

For comfort's sake, we made sure all the sharp edges of the bench were eased with sandpaper.

Innovative Deck Railings

■ BY ANDREW WORMER

One of the first decks I ever built didn't have a railing. Technically, it didn't need one because it wasn't high off the ground and didn't have stairs, but something about it always felt wrong to me. The deck looked exposed and incomplete, but I could never persuade the owners to add that railing. Maybe they thought I was looking for more work.

Not long ago, I drove by this same house, which had been bought and sold a couple of times since I worked on it. The first thing I noticed was a new deck railing on my old deck, and I realized that my intuition had been right. Although the railing itself was unremarkable, it added a real sense of completion and security to the deck. Perhaps the new owners had small children; certainly the railing would help keep babies on board. At any rate, the deck now seemed more a part of the house rather than an afterthought.

Redwood post caps and handrails balance the industrial look of steel. Although more typically used in commercial construction, steel has a strength and versatility that makes its use appropriate in this unobtrusive residential deck rail that doesn't get in the way of the view.

Battens Simplify Baluster Assembly

I wanted to build an elegant deck railing for my small bungalow in Pasadena, California, that would be simple enough for on-site construction and not involve specially milled lumber.

Because I think that the weakest part of the rail system is the joint where bottom rail meets post, I wanted the joint to remain tight and strong. Before installing the posts, I mortised them for a slip tenon, which connected to the bottom rail in an open mortise (drawing, below). This mortise allowed the rail to be dropped over the tenon and screwed to the post.

The heart of the rail system is the baluster assembly, which is simply two lengths per section of ¼-in. by 1½-in. batten cut to the length of the section. The 2x2 balusters were laid out and spaced 5½ in. o.c., and the battens nailed to the top and bottom of each created a balustrade, which could then be dropped into place on top of the bottom rail.

With a router and an adjustable fence, I next cut a plow into the center of the underside of the top rail to receive the top batten of the balusters. To finish, I installed 1-in. by 1½-in. bed molding against the balusters on both sides and under the top rail and put supports under the center of each bottom rail.

The hard part was priming and painting the railing, which took longer to do by hand than it had to build it. But this was before I bought high-volume low-pressure spray equipment, which makes finishing almost fun.

Steve Orton is a builder in Seattle, Washington.

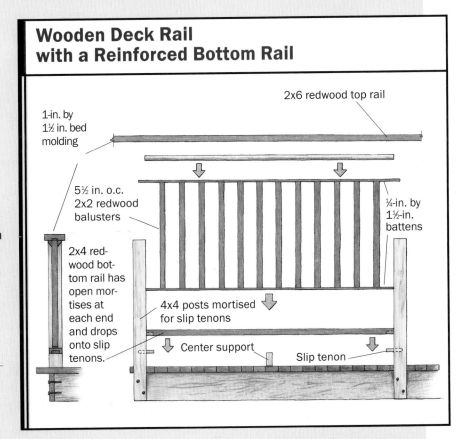

Slip tenons reinforce this redwood railing. The bottom rail on this redwood railing drops onto slip tenons mortised into the posts. The balusters are premounted onto ¼-in. by 1½-in. battens to make a balustrade that is then attached to the top and bottom rails.

Wooden Deck Rail with a Reinforced Bottom Rail

2x6 redwood top rail

1-in. by 1½ in. bed molding

5½ in. o.c. 2x2 redwood balusters

¼-in. by 1½-in. battens

2x4 redwood bottom rail has open mortises at each end and drops onto slip tenons.

4x4 posts mortised for slip tenons

Center support

Slip tenon

Cable Railings Are Strong and Unobtrusive

Any sailor can tell you that stainless-steel marine hardware will hold up well to weather, a prime consideration when choosing deck-rail material. Long used for railings and lifelines on boats, stainless-steel cable and fasteners are strong and versatile, and they don't obscure the view.

Plastic-coated stainless-steel cable can be used in conjunction with a conventionally framed post and top-rail system. In the deck railing shown on the facing page, the cable is attached to cedar posts with stainless I-bolts and threaded through holes drilled in the center post that are lined with plastic sleeves. A turnbuckle puts tension on the continuous cable.

The redwood and steel deck shown at right, designed by Eric Logan and built by Greg Pope, certainly evokes images of the sea. Custom-fabricated gray-painted steel posts are bolted directly to the steel framing, and stainless fasteners connect the cable to the posts (drawing, above). The handrail is milled from two pieces of redwood and screwed to the ¼-in. steel angle. All of the decking, the handrails, and the post caps are sealed with three coats of Sikkens® polyurethane.

Although this deck and rail were designed to meet the specifications of a childless couple, most local codes would frown on this balustrade detail because of the spacing between cables. However, the balustrade could easily be brought into compliance with minimal visual impact by adding more horizontal cables and reducing the spacing between them to 4 in.

Steel and Redwood Deck Rail

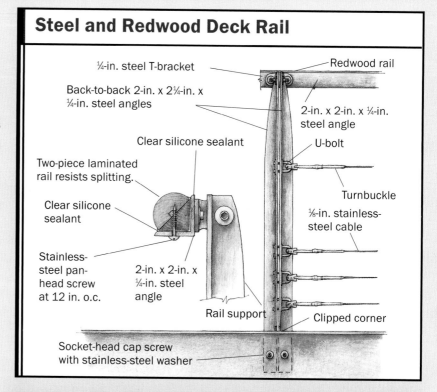

- ¼-in. steel T-bracket
- Redwood rail
- Back-to-back 2-in. x 2¼-in. x ¼-in. steel angles
- 2-in. x 2-in. x ¼-in. steel angle
- Clear silicone sealant
- U-bolt
- Two-piece laminated rail resists splitting.
- Clear silicone sealant
- Turnbuckle
- ⅛-in. stainless-steel cable
- Stainless-steel pan-head screw at 12 in. o.c.
- 2-in. x 2-in. x ¼-in. steel angle
- Rail support
- Clipped corner
- Socket-head cap screw with stainless-steel washer

A maritime feel in a central Wyoming backyard. The gray-painted steel frame, stainless marine cable and fittings, and redwood decking and handrail evoke the feel of the sea on this deck, which was designed by Eric Logan.

Good Rail Design Starts with Codes and Common Sense

In most areas, local building codes establish guidelines for rail safety. Most local codes follow the national codes, and their guidelines are easy to follow (see sidebar pp.138-139 for a summary of code requirements).

But building codes establish only minimum guidelines. Often, common sense—or intuition—is a more reliable guide. For example, Scott Schuttner, author of *Building and Designing Decks* (The Taunton Press, 1993), recommends some type of rail whenever one can fall more than the actual thickness of the deck framing. A short rail or bench can help to establish a boundary between different levels without being intrusive. Schuttner also recommends a 42-in. rather than a 36-in. rail for decks that are high off the ground for more security.

Common sense also dictates that deck railings take account of the weather. Naturally rot-resistant redwood, cedar, and cypress are good, if pricey, alternatives to pressure-treated lumber. Even steel can make a good railing.

On any wood deck railing, beveling or rounding over edges helps minimize splintering, which is especially important on a top rail that meets a lot of rumps and forearms. Making connections from underneath also helps a wood railing because it protects fastener holes from rain and snow. And maintaining the railing with an appropriate finish will help keep water out and make the wood less prone to checking.

Cedar and stainless steel stand up to weather. This gray-stained cedar railing designed by Clay Benjamin Smook uses stainless-steel fittings and plastic-coated stainless-steel marine cable in its balustrade. Plastic sleeves line drilled holes in the center post.

Although the railing was unremarkable, it added a real sense of completion and security to the deck.

Although there are lots of options when it comes to building deck railings, not all of them are good. One railing design that I've seen far too often always makes me cringe: a rickety 2x4 post-and-rail assembly with a balustrade of lumberyard-variety pressure-treated lattice. What's wrong? Although it looks substantial, the flimsy, stapled-together lattice can splinter easily, sharp points can catch little hands, and a toddler with a good head of steam can break through. On top of that, the lattice blocks the view.

For a look at the possibilities in railing materials and designs, check out the deck railings featured in this article. Although my New England roots make me partial to wood railings with full balustrades, other railings suggest the advantages of different materials and new design approaches.

Andrew Wormer is a contributing editor with Fine Homebuilding *and the author of* The Builder's Book of Bathrooms *and* Taunton's Bathroom Idea Book, *both published by The Taunton Press.*

Recycle Glass Doors for a Railing You Can See Through

On a recent project, my clients asked for a railing that wouldn't intrude on their exceptional views of the mountains that surround their vacation home. Because the deck was 18 ft. off the ground and had to withstand visits from their grandchildren, it had to be safe as well.

My solution was to use cast-off tempered safety glass salvaged from failed double-pane glass doors. Many glass companies keep these discarded panels, separate the glass, and sell the individual tempered plates for around $20 each. Measuring 76 in. by 33 in. and nearly impossible to break, this glass is ideal for railings.

The first step is to lay out the vertical posts, remembering that tempered panels can't be cut. Although a glass company can supply smaller sizes of tempered glass, the cost per square foot goes up considerably (around $6 per sq. ft. in my area), so it makes sense to lay out the posts carefully—I use 4x4 posts 90 in. o.c.—and use full-size panels wherever it's possible.

The bottom rail I use is typically a 2x4 with a support block in the middle to keep the rail rigid. The top rail is a 2x6, and the side stiles are 2x2s. I've routed out ³⁄₁₆-in.-wide by ¼-in.-deep grooves down the centers of the stiles and rails to accept the glass (bottom drawing, facing page), and I've also ripped ¾-in. by ¾-in. stops, nailed them to the stiles and rails with 4d galvanized finish nails, and set the glass that way (top drawing, facing page). Routing the stiles and rails probably requires a bit more care but results in a cleaner look. In both cases, I use beads of clear silicone around the perimeter of the glass to seal the joint against seepage and to prevent the glass from rattling in the wind.

Leave about ⅛-in. extra space in the frame for expansion, and set the glass on setting blocks (you can get them from a glass company), which keep the glass from resting directly on the framing. Check with your local building code to make sure that this detail is code compliant.

Ken Simmons is a builder in Rumney, New Hampshire.

A glass railing doesn't obscure the view. Salvaged tempered-glass panels from failed thermopane sliders make a strong and unobtrusive deck railing.

Wooden Stops Are an Easy Way to Retain Tempered-Glass Panels

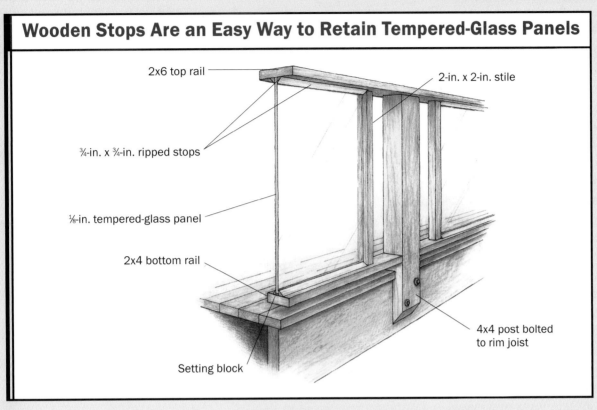

2x6 top rail

2-in. x 2-in. stile

¾-in. x ¾-in. ripped stops

⅛-in. tempered-glass panel

2x4 bottom rail

4x4 post bolted to rim joist

Setting block

Tempered-Glass Panels Set in Grooves Provide a Cleaner Look

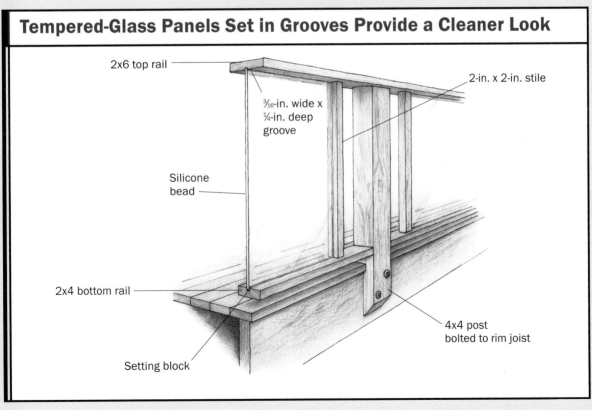

2x6 top rail

2-in. x 2-in. stile

³⁄₁₆-in. wide x ¼-in. deep groove

Silicone bead

2x4 bottom rail

4x4 post bolted to rim joist

Setting block

Lighted Railing Is Pretty and Safe at Night

Pittsburgh-area deck designer and builder Robert Viviano's technique for illuminating an outdoor newel-post/handrail system is a blend of low- and high-tech. The central component is commercially available acrylic rod that reflects light along its length from a light source mounted in the newel post.

These rods are mounted in a routed groove cut in the handrail and are usually either ½ in. by ½ in. square or ½-in. dia. round. The tubes extend into the newel post right to the light source, which is typically a 7-W fluorescent bulb that is mounted in a porcelain fixture, and function like oversize fiber optics. Another groove routed in the two-piece handrail carries electrical cable from newel to newel.

Acrylic rods help to light the way. Inset into the handrails, solid acrylic rods reflect light from fluorescent fixtures concealed in the newel posts.

Lighted Newel Post and Rail

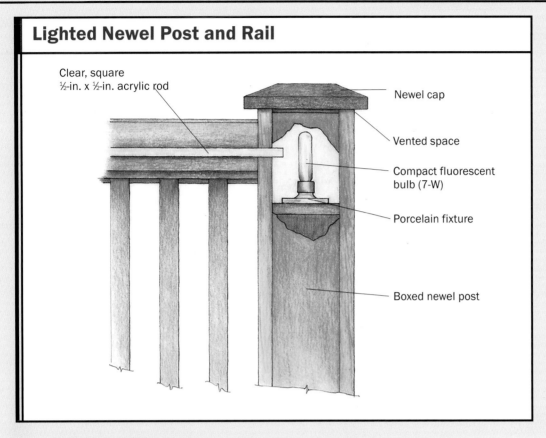

Clear, square
½-in. x ½-in. acrylic rod

Newel cap

Vented space

Compact fluorescent
bulb (7-W)

Porcelain fixture

Boxed newel post

Cross Section of Lighted Rail

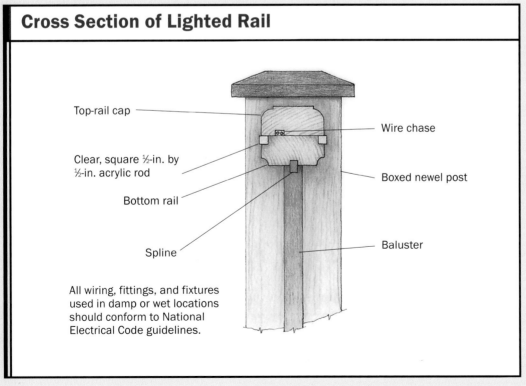

Top-rail cap

Wire chase

Clear, square ½-in. by
½-in. acrylic rod

Boxed newel post

Bottom rail

Spline

Baluster

All wiring, fittings, and fixtures
used in damp or wet locations
should conform to National
Electrical Code guidelines.

Code Requirements for Deck-Rail Safety

Most building codes require a guardrail when a deck is more than 30 in. above the ground and a handrail whenever there are more than two risers on a stairway. Guardrail height by code is usually a minimum of 36 in., and handrail height should be between 34 in. and 38 in. If there is a bottom rail on the guardrail, it should be no more than 2 in. off the deck.

Spacing between the components of a rail system should be no more than 4 in. (except at the tread, where a 6-in. opening is okay), which means that a ball 4 in. in diameter shouldn't be able to pass through the rail. Although that may seem to be a pretty small opening, children have been known to get into (and through) some pretty small spaces.

The grip size of a stairway handrail should have a circular cross section with a diameter between 1¼ in. and 2 in. Other handrail profiles are possible, but the largest cross-sectional dimension should not exceed 2¼ in., and the perimeter dimension should fall between 4 in. and 6¼ in. The essential concern for the handrail is graspability; a rail design that is appropriate on the guardrail of the deck may be inappropriate on the handrail of the stairway.

Code-Approvable Handrail Sections

Other profiles are approvable as long as they meet graspability requirements.

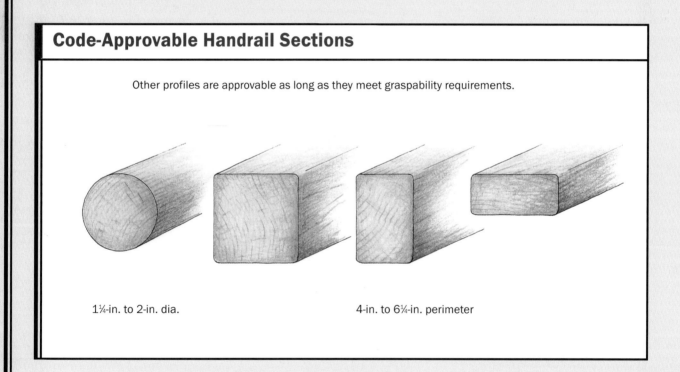

1¼-in. to 2-in. dia.　　　　　4-in. to 6¼-in. perimeter

Handrail and Guardrail Guidelines

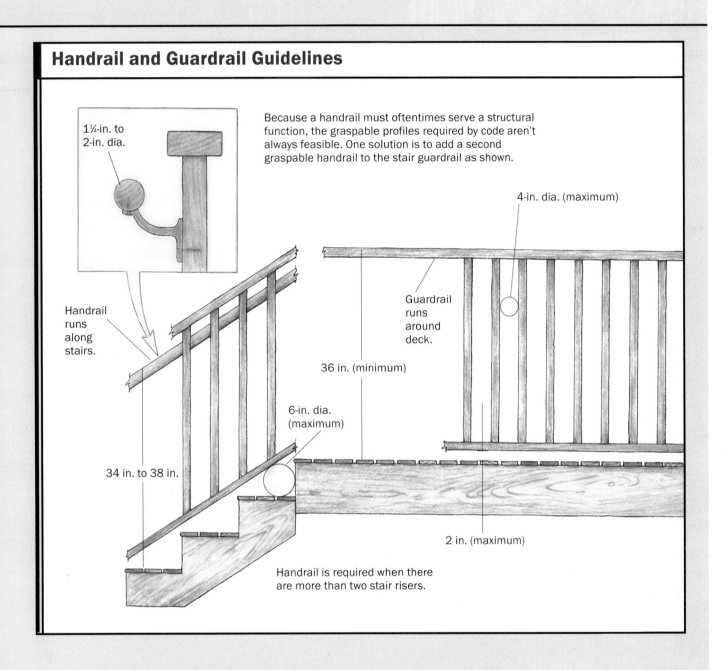

1¼-in. to 2-in. dia.

Because a handrail must oftentimes serve a structural function, the graspable profiles required by code aren't always feasible. One solution is to add a second graspable handrail to the stair guardrail as shown.

4-in. dia. (maximum)

Handrail runs along stairs.

Guardrail runs around deck.

36 in. (minimum)

6-in. dia. (maximum)

34 in. to 38 in.

2 in. (maximum)

Handrail is required when there are more than two stair risers.

A Furniture-Grade Deck

■ BY SCOTT FLEMING

Hungry deer prowl the sunburned hills of Danville, California. When spring rolls around and flowerbeds full of tender sprouts make their annual push, the deer practically paw the ground in anticipation. But not at Steve and Celeste Butterfield's house.

On their steep hillside, the Butterfields had grown weary of feeding the deer a steady diet of pedigreed plants with Latin names. The only shrubs that the deer wouldn't eat were the ones they couldn't reach—like the ones in pots out on the decaying deck. Deer don't like stairs, or wooden floors for that matter.

Landscaping seemed like a losing proposition, so Steve and Celeste decided to put their outdoor-improvement money into replacing the old deck. They hired me to lavish attention on the new deck as though it were a piece of furniture and to make it last by avoiding the mistakes made in their original deck.

With quality materials and finely detailed design elements, this multi-level deck was built to last.

Why Decks Go Bad

The Butterfields' original deck didn't have much of a chance at longevity. Its deck boards were too close together, and the oak leaves that collected in the narrow crevices between the boards held moisture and promoted rot. The deck's ledger was nailed directly to the plywood siding, and the lack of an airspace caused rot both in ledger and in plywood. At the butt joints between the deck boards, nails, too close to the board ends, caused splits and potentially dangerous slivers that angled upward toward oncoming feet.

At our earliest design sessions, we nailed down the important details to be included in the new deck. It would be made of the best-quality redwood that we could find, and it would be detailed to shed water and to promote ventilation. All exposed edges would be rounded to make them soft to the eye and to the touch, and all decking fasteners would be hidden from view. The railing would be unobtrusive and include a discreet lighting system. Finally, a pair of stairways to the hillside below would make for easy access to the area under the deck. With these marching orders, I set out to design and build the ultimate deck.

Following the Lay of the Land

The new deck would be made of the best-quality redwood that we could find, and it would be detailed to shed water and to promote ventilation.

As the defunct deck was being torn down and hauled off, Barry Pfaff and I began the layout for the new one. The old deck was 10 ft. wide, and we all agreed that a wider deck would be a more useful deck. We settled on 12 ft., which leaves enough room to have a table and chairs on the deck with circulation space to the sides.

As shown in the drawing, the deck wraps around two sides of the house, with a couple of triangular bays that are 20 in. below the main deck. The bays serve several functions.

First, their triangular shapes are inherently strong, adding diagonal bracing to the horizontal plane of the deck. Second, we didn't want to cut any of the limbs of the splendid oaks that ring the house. By lowering the bays, we could project the deck into the treetops without pruning any limbs, which gives the bays a cozy, tree house feeling. Finally, the bay on the east side of the house is also the landing for the two stairways that lead to grade. By code, the stairs can't have more than 18 risers in a single run. By lowering the landing, we could take the stairs down to grade in straight runs.

A Wraparound Deck

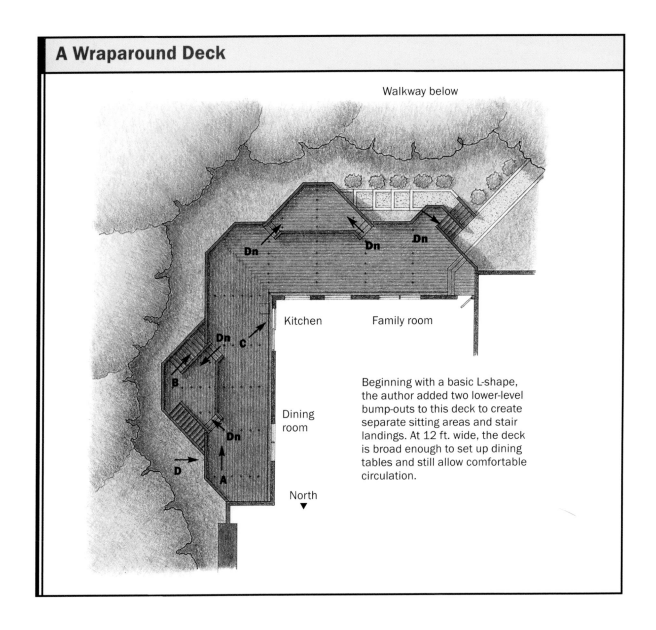

Walkway below

Dn · Dn · Dn

Kitchen · Family room

Dn · C

B

Dining room

Dn

D · A

North ▼

Beginning with a basic L-shape, the author added two lower-level bump-outs to this deck to create separate sitting areas and stair landings. At 12 ft. wide, the deck is broad enough to set up dining tables and still allow comfortable circulation.

Don't Forget the Space Under the Deck

Two conditions made it tough to get around under the original deck. A forest of posts and diagonal braces made an obstacle course out of the hillside next to the house. And the clay soil turned to grease during the rainy season. Steve and Celeste wanted an easy-to-use path under the deck. So before we got into carpentry, we did our time as concrete workers.

First we poured stepped concrete grade beams that roughly follow the perimeter of the deck. The grade beams are 4 ft. apart, and in several places they are affixed to the deck piers by tie beams. In combination with pressure-treated 2x12s, these tie beams double as risers for a path that steps down the hill in 4-ft. sq. increments.

The walkway connects the three stair landings and the door to the utility room below the deck. We filled the path's 4-ft.-sq. cells with smooth, 2-in. blue pebbles and spread a layer of gravel on the soil underneath the deck.

Pathway as retaining wall. Stepped concrete grade beams under the deck create a terrace of steps that help stabilize the hillside. Photo taken at B on floor plan.

Pressure-Treated Lumber Gets Special Care

We used the old concrete piers wherever possible to support the new deck. By using some 6x12s and several custom-made ⅜-in. steel brackets, we were able to pick up almost all of the loads from the new, expanded deck. Only four additional piers were required, mostly where the new deck had multiple levels.

All the new posts, beams, and joists are Douglas fir and have been treated with ACZA preservative. I guess the companies that apply the preservative to this lumber search out the lowest grades of structural material, reasoning that it will all end up out of sight someplace. Not here. We combed through the piles of treated lumber, searching with little success for straight sticks with no twist. To fix the pieces we ended up using, we had to break some new ground, prepwise. We ran pressure-treated posts and joists over a jointer. This unlikely scenario was especially important for the deck joists, which all had wicked crowns. On a job such as this, with fastidious clients who wanted straight, true lines of deck boards, there really wasn't any other way to go. We had to change knives six times before we were through jointing the stuff.

We chamfered all visible edges of the posts and recoated all the pressure-treated material with a copper-based wood preservative to even out the color. This color turned out to match the trunks of the indigenous live oak and tan oak quite nicely, so the substructure of the deck virtually disappears.

Hidden Fasteners Anchor the Decking

Back at the shop, we prepared the 6-in.-wide deck boards for installation. They are mostly 20-footers, which started out at a true, rough-sawn 2-in. thickness. We surfaced them down to 1¾ in. thick and radiused their top edges with a ⅜-in. roundover bit. On site, the indefatigable Lalo Arjona cut the deck boards to length, radiused their ends, and then coated them, top and bottom, with Penofin® from Performance Coatings Inc. This preservative is specially formulated for redwood. It has some reddish pigment in it, but not enough to impart the chalky, orange color that some stains leave on redwood.

We spaced the deck boards a generous ¼ in. apart. Large gaps make it easier to keep the deck clean but can trap spike heels. (Of course, a redwood deck is not the place to wear high heels, as Steve and Celeste would be quick to point out.)

The decking is affixed to the joists from below by way of 22-in. Deckmaster® deck clips. These sheet-metal clips are T-shaped in section. The top of the T is attached to the top of its joist, where it also serves as a flange for screwing the deck boards from below (photo, bottom left) with 1½-in. galvanized deck screws. The flanges elevate the deck boards slightly above the joists, promoting air circulation.

The deck wraps around the corner of the house in a series of herringbone steps. At this strategic corner, equidistant to both ends of the deck, we placed a basket covered by a trap door to house a length of garden hose (photo, bottom right).

One deck board out from the house, a band of ebonized redwood borders the edge of the deck. The strong line established by the ebonized strip draws your attention away from the tapered deck board next to it, made necessary by the out-of-square corner of the house. Incidentally, ebonized wood has simply been coated with black stain.

Ebonized redwood diamonds add another decorative touch to the deck. They are ¾ in. thick, and they are held in place by a single plugged screw. The diamonds occur over joists, between deck boards to ensure good drainage. After the deck boards had been installed, we cut the recesses for the diamonds with a bearing-guided router following a pattern clamped to the deck.

Hidden fasteners attach deck boards. Galvanized-steel angles affixed to the joists provide a flange for screws driven from below.

Housing the garden hose. A wire basket topped with a trap door conceals the hose. Behind it, a band of ebonized redwood borders the deck. Photo taken at C on floor plan.

Railing Sections Include Circular Cutouts

The railing design includes a horizontal 2x6 that's halfway between the 3x6 railing cap and the deck. The 2x6 has round or oval cutouts flanking a diamond-shaped recess in the middle. Semicircular cutouts at each end create the prongs that connect to the posts. Above and below the 2x6s, a pair of 1-in. copper pipes on 4½-in. centers complete the railing.

The post-to-post distances were kept under 48 in. to minimize deflection. We cut the copper to length with a zero-hook blade on a chopsaw. Short sections of the pipe worked fine as dowels to join 2x6 railing sections with the posts.

The circular cutouts on the wooden railing sections begin on the drill press with a 2½-in. hole bored with a Forstner bit. The 1⅛-in. holes in the end grain were bored with a horizontal milling machine.

Next, a bandsaw removes the waste from the rail ends.

Short sections of copper pipe act as dowels to connect the rails with their posts.

Low-Voltage Wiring Is Concealed in the Railings

There are 108 posts in the railing of this deck, and each one has a minimum of six holes drilled in it for bolts and for the 1-in. copper pipes that serve as railings. To ensure accuracy and to speed things up as much as possible, all the holes were bored in the shop using a drill press fitted with a fixture to hold the posts in the right place (top photo, p. 146).

At less than 4 ft., the 1-in. copper pipe is plenty sturdy to be a railing on a deck. It is also light, durable, splinter-free and easy to install. And although gaudy in its initial brightness, the copper rails slowly oxidize to a soft reddish brown that is compatible with redwood. The copper rails barely affect the view on this deck, and they are maintenance free.

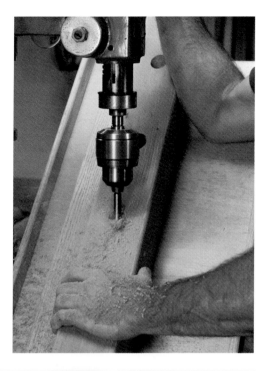

Fabricating posts. With the post fixed at the correct angle, mortises for the 1-in. copper pipe rails were bored with a 1⅛-in. Forstner bit.

The copper pipe also serves as a conduit for a 12-V lighting system. A 700-W transformer in the utility room powers 40 lamps, 30 of which illuminate the deck and stairs. The remaining 10 are on the walkway below. We pulled the wires for the lighting as we assembled the railing section by section, drilling out the posts in the appropriate spots for the lamps.

The Railings End at Curvy Posts

On your basic California deck, a 2x6 cap rail covers 4x4 posts. Cap sections abut atop the posts, where they are nailed into the end grain of the posts. After a couple of seasons in the sun and rain, the cap rails split around the nails. It's ugly.

On the Butterfields' deck, the cap-rail sections meet in midair between posts that are 4 in. apart. They are held together by dovetailed splines made of Honduras mahogany that have been soaked in Penofin until they were slippery enough to drive into their dovetailed slots. The rails end at the stairs, where built-up posts of 4x4s flair out, Deco style, to catch the ends of the cap rails.

By the way, a deck like this needs regular maintenance. The Butterfields give it an annual coat of Penofin for protection from the sun and rain. When we started, Penofin still contained VOC solvents, which have now been outlawed by California's air-quality laws. The new formulation, according to Steve and Celeste, seems to work just as well as the old one.

Scott Fleming is a builder/designer who lives in Honolulu, Hawaii, and owns Sansea Design/Consulting.

Curved posts meet straight stairs. Held together by dovetailed splines, curvy posts made of three sections of 4x4 anchor the balustrade at stair landings. The posts nest in shallow mortises in the underside of the cap rail. Photo taken at D on floor plan.

Fantail Deck Stairs

■ BY JOSE L. FLORESCA

I started working with curves about 10 years ago. I learned from a master carpenter, Tom Pratt, who taught me how to build curved forms for concrete pools. What made this different from rectilinear construction was that we used plywood for the top and bottom plates. To follow the different radii for the curved surfaces of the pool, we cut the plates with a jigsaw or a bandsaw. A similar technique worked when I built a circular soffit in my kitchen. But my appetite for challenging curved projects hadn't been really nourished since Pratt moved out of town in 1987.

A new challenge presented itself when my partner, Steve Cassella, and I saw the

The seven stringers, fanned out from an axis, and the band-sawn treads on this exterior staircase gave the author and his partner an opportunity to depart from the common world of rectilinear carpentry.

plans for a remodel/deck addition designed by Dwayne Kohler that included a set of exterior stairs that fanned out in a quadrant, or quarter circle. Questions arose about the stair's construction: How many stringers are necessary to support the treads? How should the stringers be supported? What kind of calculations would be necessary to build the stairway?

After we got the job, and before we could build the quadrant stairs, we first enlarged the home's existing upper deck and built a new lower deck. That was the easy part of the job.

Calculations and Cogitations

The plans called for a straight set of stringers to run from the upper deck down to a landing. From the landing a second set of stringers would fan out in a quadrant. The total rise of the stairway—from upper deck to lower—is 93 in. We divided the height into 12 risers. More risers would have meant more treads, resulting in longer stringers. And longer stringers would have taken up more space on the lower deck. The rise (93 in.) divided by the number of risers (12)

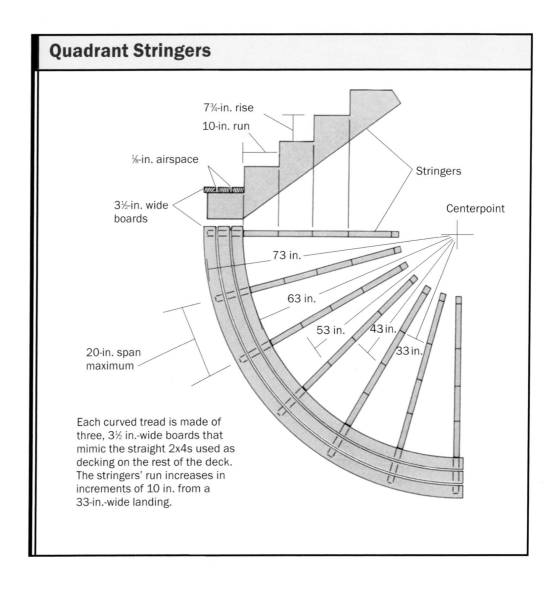

Quadrant Stringers

7¾-in. rise
10-in. run
⅛-in. airspace
3½-in. wide boards
Stringers
Centerpoint
73 in.
63 in.
53 in.
43 in.
33 in.
20-in. span maximum

Each curved tread is made of three, 3½ in.-wide boards that mimic the straight 2x4s used as decking on the rest of the deck. The stringers' run increases in increments of 10 in. from a 33-in.-wide landing.

gave us an individual riser height of 7¾ in. We cut 10-in. treads because 10 in. is a good tread width for three 2x4s with ⅛-in. drainage space between the boards and a ¼-in. nosing.

After we determined the length of our stringers, we framed the landing and installed the straight-run stringers to the upper deck. We could now concentrate on the quadrant stairs.

The calculations for cutting the stringers of the quadrant stairs are the same as those for the straight run above. The big question was how many stringers did we need to support the treads? We decided that the span between the stringers at their widest point (the outside edge of the bottom riser) should not exceed 20 in. because the grain of the treads is not consistently perpendicular to all of the stringers they rest on.

The landing is 33 in. wide. We used this dimension as the radius for the top risers of the quadrant stair stringers. Because our treads are 10 in. wide, the radii for the other risers are larger in 10-in. increments (the width of each tread); i.e., 43 in., 53 in., 63 in. and 73 in.

To calculate the number of stringers for the bottom step, we first had to calculate the circumference of the circle formed by the radius of the bottom step. Knowing that $2\pi r$ = circumference (r is the radius), we plugged in the numbers: 2 x 3.1416 x 73 = 458.6736 in. The stairs occupy a quarter circle, so we divided the circumference by four. This figure was divided by the desired stringer span, 20 in., which gave us the number of 20-in. spaces in the quarter circle. Rounding our quotient to the nearest whole number gave us six spaces, so we'd need seven stringers.

All the stringers are supported by a single, curved brace, which was notched to accommodate each stringer. A 2x10 leg runs between the deck joist and the brace.

A Curved Brace for the Stringers

Installing the stringers posed yet another challenge. How should we support the tops of the stringers? Rather than support each stringer individually, I visualized a single, curved brace that each stringer would bear against.

I cut the brace from a 2x12. The curve of the brace is a segment of a circle. Its radius was determined by finding a centerpoint that was perpendicular to the center stringer and equidistant to the backs of all the other stringers, roughly 3 in. from their tops. We added 1 in. to the circle's radius to allow the brace to be notched around each stringer for lateral support. The brace was attached to the framing in such a way that its face is perpendicular to the back of the center stringer (photo, above). A 2x10 leg supports the curved brace and was nailed to the top of one of the deck's joists. The top of the leg

Rather than support each stringer individually, I visualized a single, curved brace that each stringer would bear against.

The calculations for determining rise and run for the stringers for the quadrant staircase are identical to ones used on conventional, parallel stairs. The stringers differ from the ordinary in that they radiate from a common point.

was cut at a compound angle and nailed to the curved brace (photo, above). With both pieces nailed in place, we then notched the curved brace with a jigsaw to accommodate the stringers.

The bottoms of the stringers sit on the lower deck and are toenailed in place. To provide nailing for the landing's deck boards, we added blocking between the stringers about 3 in. behind the top risers.

Determining Tread Length

To calculate the length of the treads along their circumference, we multiplied the radius of the lowest riser by two to get its diameter. We then multiplied this diameter by π (3.1416) to obtain the circumference. Because the arc of the stairway is a quarter circle, we divided the circumference by four.

For each of the four treads, it was necessary to cut three rows of boards (to simulate 2x4s): the inner board, which butts up against the riser above; the middle board; and the outer board whose nose hangs over the riser below. Each board of each tread has both an inside and an outside radius. The inside radius of the inner board is the same as the radius of the riser above—33 in., 43 in., 53 in., etc. The outside radius of each board is always 3½ in. (the width of a 2x4) greater than the inside radius. The inside radius of the next concentric tread board is greater by ⅛ in. (airspace) than the outside radius of the previous tread.

To calculate the lumber necessary for the treads, we used the same formula as that used to determine tread length. We calculated for each of the 12 tread boards plus one for the quarter-circle edge on the landing. To our total lengths we added an additional

Three 3½-in-wide curved boards make up each tread. The curves were laid out using a marking device made out of a 1x2, an adhesive-backed tape measure, and a set of trammel points. After layout, the authors cut the boards on a bandsaw.

10% as a safety factor. We added it up and purchased tight-knot cedar 2x10s in this linear quantity. Although this figure was derived as a length along a curve, it allotted for additional material needed so that we could stagger joints on the stringers.

Marking and Cutting the Treads

Accuracy was essential, so we laid out the curved treads on the level floor of our cabinet shop. Steve made a marking device out of a 1x2, an adhesive-backed tape measure, and a set of trammel points. One point was set at zero. The other was adjusted to the lengths of the curves determined when we calculated the tread lengths (drawing, p. 148). When marking the curves on the 2x10s, we avoided using checked ends, and we placed knots so as not to create holes or cracks.

We first cut the curves with a jigsaw, which was inadequate because the cuts were not consistently square. The bandsaw cut the curves, but it became a two-man job because of the long lengths involved. We left the ends of the boards long and cut them to length during installation. We routed a ¼-in. radius on all visible edges.

Installing the treads was fairly straight forward. We predrilled the nail holes where necessary so that we wouldn't split the ends, and we staggered the joints.

Curved work has a natural character to it. It adds life to the otherwise rectangular dimensions of most carpentry. Enter some geometry, a bandsaw, and—voila—quadrant stairs.

José L. Floresca is a carpenter in Seattle, Washington. Steve Cassella co-authored this article.

Accuracy was essential, so we laid out the curved treads on the level floor of our cabinet shop.

CREDITS

The articles compiled in this book appeared in the following issues of *Fine Homebuilding:*

p. iii: Photo © Jacek Bogucki.

Table of contents: Photos on p. iv (left) © Kevin M. Mahoney; (right) by Jefferson Kolle, courtesy *Fine Homebuilding,* © The Taunton Press, Inc.; p. 1 by Andy Engel, courtesy *Fine Homebuilding,* © The Taunton Press, Inc.

p. 4: Two Lessons from a Porch Addition by James C. C. Rice, issue 88. Photos on pp.4 (large) and 10 by Rich Ziegner, courtesy of *Fine Homebuilding,* © The Taunton Press, Inc.; pp. 4 (inset), 7, and 9 © James C. C. Rice. Illustrations by Bob Goodfellow, © The Taunton Press, Inc..

p. 11: Porches That Won't Rot by Kevin M. Mahoney, issue 81. Photos © Kevin M. Mahoney. Illustrations by Bob Goodfellow, © The Taunton Press, Inc.

p. 18: Building a Grand Veranda by Kevin Wilkes, issue 132. Photos on pp. 18 and 22 by Roe A. Osborn, courtesy of *Fine Homebuilding,* © The Taunton Press, Inc.; p. 20 Jim Black. Illustrations by Vince Babak, © The Taunton Press, Inc.

p. 24: A Screened-Porch Addition by Jerry Germer, issue 72. Photos by Vincent Laurence, courtesy of *Fine Homebuilding,* © The Taunton Press, Inc. Illustration © Bob LaPointe.

p. 28: A Builder's Screen Porch by Scott McBride, issue 86. Photos on pp. 28, 29 (bottom), 30–34, and 35 (bottom) © Scott McBride; pp. 29 (top) and 35 (top) by Jefferson Kolle, courtesy of *Fine Homebuilding,* © The Taunton Press, Inc. Illustrations by Bob Goodfellow, © The Taunton Press, Inc.

p. 36: A Screen Porch Dresses Up a Ranch by Alex L. Varga, issue 96. Photos on pp. 37, 41 and 43 by Rich Ziegner, courtesy of *Fine Homebuilding,* © The Taunton Press, Inc.; p. 40 © Alex L. Varga. Illustration by Bob La Pointe, © The Taunton Press, Inc.

p. 44: Adding a Seasonal Porch by Ken Textor, issue 103. Photos by Steve Culpepper, courtesy of *Fine Homebuilding,* © The Taunton Press, Inc. Illustrations by Christopher Clapp, © The Taunton Press, Inc.

p. 51: Deck Design by Scott Grove, issue 29. Photos © Scott Grove. Illustrations © Frances Ashforth.

p. 61: Choosing Materials for Exterior Decks by Scott Gibson, issue 132. Photos on p. 61, by Scott Gibson, courtesy of *Fine Homebuilding,* © The Taunton Press, Inc.; pp. 62–68 by Scott Phillips, courtesy of *Fine Homebuilding,* © The Taunton Press, Inc.

p. 70: Controlling Moisture in Deck Lumber by Bob Falk, Kent McDonald and Jerry Winandy, issue 97. Photos on pp. 70, 71, 72 (left), and 73 © Steve Schmieding, Jim Vargo, Bob Falk, Kent McDonald, and Jerry Winandy; p. 72 (right) courtesy of The Southern Forest Products Association.

p. 74: Details for a Lasting Deck by Bob Falk and Sam Williams, issue 102. Photos © Bob Falk and Sam Williams. Illustrations by Vince Babak, © The Taunton Press, Inc.

p. 82: Getting a Deck Off to a Good Start by Peter J. Bilodeau, issue 122. Photos by Andy Engel, courtesy of *Fine Homebuilding,* © The Taunton Press, Inc. Illustrations by Dan Thornton, © The Taunton Press, Inc.

p. 88: The Care and Feeding of Wooden Decks by Jon Tobey, issue 138. Photos on pp. 88, 90–93, and 95 by Tom O'Brien, courtesy of *Fine Homebuilding,* © The Taunton Press, Inc.; p. 94 © Rhonda Kelly.

p. 96: Building a Curved Deck with Synthetic Decking by Ted Putnam, issue 111. Photos on p.96 by Charles Bickford, courtesy of *Fine Homebuilding,* © The Taunton Press, Inc.; pp. 98, 99 (bottom), 100–102 © Ted Putnam; p. 99 (top and center) by Scott Phillips, courtesy of *Fine Homebuilding,* © The Taunton Press, Inc.

p. 103: Railing against the Elements by Scott McBride, issue 70. Photos on p. 103 by Kevin Ireton, courtesy of *Fine Homebuilding,* © The Taunton Press, Inc.; pp. 105 and 109 © Scott McBride. Illustrations by Bob Goodfellow, © The Taunton Press, Inc.

p. 110: Exterior-Trim Details That Last by John Michael Davis, issue 141. Photos by Tom O'Brien, courtesy of *Fine Homebuilding,* © The Taunton Press, Inc. Illustrations by Christopher Clapp, © The Taunton Press, Inc.

p. 119: Learning Curves for Decks by Scott Padgett, issue 144. Photos on pp. 119 and 120 (top right), and 124 by Andy Engel, courtesy of *Fine Homebuilding,* © The Taunton Press, Inc.; pp. 120 (top left and bottom), 121, and 123 © Scott Padgett; pp. 122, 125, and 126 © Richard Lackey. Illustrations by Dan Thornton, © The Taunton Press, Inc.

p. 127: A Comfortable Outdoor Bench by David Bright, issue 82. Photos by Charles Miller, courtesy of *Fine Homebuilding,* © The Taunton Press, Inc. Illustration by Chuck Lockhart, © The Taunton Press, Inc.

p. 130: Innovative Deck Railings by Andrew Wormer, issue 104. Photos on pp. 130 and 132 © Jacek Bogucki; p. 131 © Dean Della Ventura; p. 133 © Anton Grassl; pp. 134 and 136 by Andrew Wormer, courtesy of *Fine Homebuilding,* © The Taunton Press, Inc. Illustrations by Christopher Clapp, © The Taunton Press, Inc.

p. 140: A Furniture Grade Deck by Scott Fleming, issue 106. Photos on pp. 140, 143, 144, and 146 (bottom) by Charles Miller, courtesy of *Fine Homebuilding,* © The Taunton Press, Inc.; p. 145 and 146 (top) © Rosina Whitney. Illustration by Vince Babak, © The Taunton Press, Inc.

p. 147: Fantail Deck Stairs by Jose L. Floresca, issue 83. Photos on p. 147 © Tom McMackin; pp. 149–151 © Jose L. Floresca. Illustration by Bob Goodfellow, © The Taunton Press, Inc.

INDEX